GOD MOST POWERFUL

Other Works by Fr. Amorth
Published by Sophia Institute Press

An Exorcist Explains the Demonic
Father Amorth: My Battle against Satan
Stronger Than Evil
The Devil Is Afraid of Me
Get Behind Me, Satan

GOD MOST POWERFUL

An Exorcist's Testament to God's Victory Over the Devil

Father Gabriele Amorth

Interview with Angelo De Simone

Translated by Nicholas Reitzug

SOPHIA INSTITUTE PRESS
Manchester, New Hampshire

Contents

"Run to What Attracts You"

"The Gospel, St. Paul, Our Lady urge me on.... My aim is to draw those who read and reflect upon their own lives to place it in harmony with the purpose for which God created them."[1]

I LIVE IN THE same religious community to which the Italian exorcist Fr. Gabriele Amorth[2] belongs. Amorth is well-known, both here and throughout the world.

The memories of those who frequent him remain impressed with images of an old priest in his black cassock, stained and singed perhaps, presumably from some infernal scorching. What sticks in my mind is his large face, his well-shaved head, and the pile of letters on his desk. His jokes echo in my ears, spoken in his Bolognese accent, as effervescent as the Lambrusco they serve there; and what's more, I recall his voice as he gave his daily salutations to each of his "fine little companions" around the coffee maker.

Many believe that he sought out the devil above all in those who were presumed or truly possessed. Indeed, the literature on exorcisms tends to emphasize the role of the rebellious angel. However, Fr. Gabriele exudes a benevolent lightheartedness — both paternal and friendly — conveying that his true concern was to offer a

---

[1]   Gabriele Amorth with Paul Rodari, *The Last Exorcist: My Battle Against Satan* (Milan: Piemme, 2012), 7, 9.

[2]   For his biographical profile, see the appendix.

Fr. Gabriele Amorth was appointed exorcist in the Diocese of Rome by Cardinal Ugo Poletti in 1986.

glimpse of the kindness of the good God who holds the devil in check. In his ministry as an exorcist, his "professional" focus was, of course, on the devil, against whom he fought through prayer, scorn, holy water, and exorcisms. Yet, in reality, within those afflicted souls, he sought the divine "image and likeness" that no demonic power could ever erase. In the end, he took it as a given that God is more present, more filled with goodness, more beautiful, and more compelling than the devil.

Of course, that is true, but the religious fundamentalism of our time does a disservice to God, obscuring his benevolent and tolerant maternal and paternal nature — it makes him, so to speak, appear harsh and unkind. Fundamentalists depict him as if he had a heart of stone, from which the tablets of divine law were carved. Since they invoke God's name without making him attractive, they impose him on others without truly understanding him. As a result, they judge the "infidels" without offering them liberation and inspire fear and estrangement from the divine Creator, lacking both soul and genuine commitment to God.

God is made to seem so unappealing that he leaves a bitter taste in the soul, which then curdles into bile. Paradoxically, this can lead one to side more with the devil than with God. This, our renowned exorcist maintains, is one reason why so few radiant souls walk the sweet paths of encountering God.

In fact, he believes that many of those labeled as "possessed" are actually wounded individuals, bearing deep scars in their souls because they focus solely on God's law without ever having tasted his love. Many believe themselves to be possessed by the devil simply because they do not "feel" God as a Father. For this reason, our dear Brother considers these afflicted souls to be lost sons, wayward sheep, crucified people who have never experienced the gratuitousness of divine love. One truly becomes a son upon realizing that the origin of one's existence is neither chance nor necessity, but a free decision — an act of love, both human and divine.

Moved by priestly attention and charity, Fr. Amorth invites them therefore to rediscover within them (despite their limits) their identity, dignity, and sacrality as sons of God. It is thanks to his liberating identity as a beloved son of God that Fr. Gabriele is able to confront the devil, having received the strength and divine grace to outdo him in authority.

"It is, therefore a good, just, and useful matter," he recommends, "to proclaim in a book how our Lord is absolutely *more beautiful and more attractive than the devil.* My previous books were rather 'descriptive' of the devil, of the occult phenomena, of demonic possessions, of exorcisms and other matters of this sort. In these pages I place Our Lord front and center, for good reason, in a way that attracts our attention to him to distract us from evil. In fact, 'it is the interior attraction of the Father that arouses faith.'"[3]

And as regards the priority of attraction, he recalls what St. Augustine taught: "You show a green branch to a sheep and he follows you. You show a young boy some walnuts, and he is attracted and runs after whatever attracts him: he is attracted by love, he is attracted without suffering physical constraints, he is attracted by the link that binds the heart."[4]

Therefore, in this book, Fr. Amorth relegates the devil to a mere postscript — off the field, so to speak — just as he always did in his ministry as an exorcist.

As concerns the devil strictly speaking, in this work, the author refers for the most part to his ministry and to the books he has written, drawing from them whatever is essential.

---

[3] *La Verità Vi Farà Liberi: Catechismo degli Adulti* [*Catechism for Adults*], 194.
[4] *Liturgy of the Hours* IV, 349.

The writing of this work began with encounters and interviews. I presented our dear confrere, to whom I am grateful for the trust he granted me, the first draft written from the interviews; he read the manuscript, added to it, and then approved its final editing in form and content, as agreed by both of us.

This is the reason the book bears his name and surname with full rights on the cover and can be read as his spiritual testament.

Angelo De Simone

*Gabriele Amorth was ordained a priest on
January 24, 1954, in the Society of St. Paul.*

GOD MOST POWERFUL

CHAPTER ONE

Our God

*"Man can be grateful for God's many benefits but he cannot
thank Him as long as he is afraid, because those with
servile fear certainly do not allow themselves to be loved by
the Creator of the human race nor do they love Him."*[5]

How does religion "harmonize" man with God?

I shall get straight to the point. Every human being knows that, in
general, he cannot always manage to face reality — let alone when
struck by a terminal illness! Despair takes hold. In such tragic situ-
ations, we all become religious in a way, making "promises to a
saint" — in this case, a good doctor. And if the doctor is not enough,
we turn to God.

Is the fundamentalism of some religions diabolical?

We cannot ignore the fact that religions impose ideological bur-
dens on people, provoking strong reactions against the intolerance
and impositions they endure. This often leads to rebellion, transgression, the rejection of God, and both theoretical and practical
atheism. In this way, fundamentalism drives a wedge between
the world, humanity, and God — and for this reason, the devil
is at work.

---

[5]   Gregory the Great, *Moralia* on Job 9:64, in *Opera*, vol. 1 (Rome: Città
Nuova, 1994), 86–87.

Explain this.

The various forms of religious ideology at large disfigure the face of God and the sacrality of the human being because they seek to "oblige" God, as if God had need of us and not vice versa. On the contrary, St. Paul clarifies to the Athenians, as we read in the Acts of the Apostles, that God is not at the mercy of men, as if he were in need of something.

One deduces that religious ideology not only is not capable of liberating and elevating the human being, but indeed turns out to be harmful, an obstacle, an inhibition to revelation and the experience of the true God.

The provocations of modern religious fundamentalism thus compel a reexamination of the very concept of religion, as well as of religious language and practice. All religions should undertake an examination of conscience and ask themselves whether they are truly concerned with the real God and the happiness of man — or with something else entirely.

What can be saved from religion and from religions?

I must begin by saying how difficult it is to find the needle in the haystack of religions in general, due to the multiplicity of experiences and information about them. Nevertheless, I try to perceive what might be valid and good in what the various religions say about God.

I have come to the conclusion, however, that religions cannot say all the truth about God, precisely because *God is God*. Therefore, *they must not impose Him* on their faithful. I repeat however, that in the various expressions of religion and culture, it is a given that we find elements of truth concerning God.

Can you mention one religion in particular?

In Hinduism, for example, the most widespread religion in India, we find that "the concept of God as a transcendent and ineffable Mystery or as a personal Being is undoubtedly lofty," as we read in number 590 of the *Catechism of Adults*. "Admirable is the primacy given to the spiritual life, especially in contrast to the materialism and secularism of the West. … Noble is their ethical system and their passionate pursuit of definitive salvation. … Generous is their spirit of tolerance toward other religions. … Profound and joyful experiences of personal love for God bear fruit in ways similar to those of Christian saints," as expressed in this splendid prayer by the seventeenth-century poet Tukaram: "You [Lord] hold my hand and guide me firmly, always and everywhere present at my side. As I walk along leaning on you, you carry my heavy load. … I recognize in every man a friend, in every encounter a relative. Like a happy child, I happily play in your dear world, O God."[6]

Or another, composed in Tamil by the mystic Appar: "You are to me, O Lord, father and mother. You are all the relatives I need. You are the beloved. You are my precious treasure. You are my home, my friends, my family. You give me life and joy. I throw away all the false goods of the world. O Pearl, O Wealth, you are my All."[7]

What can be said about Islam?

"The correct attitude of man before God as submission, obedience, and trusting surrender characterizes Islam," as we are reminded in number 599 of the *Catechism of Adults*. Their faith is expressed in the

---

[6]   Olivier Lacombe, "Brahminism," in *Mysticism and Mystics: The 'Nucleus' of the Great Religions and Spiritual Disciplines* (Cinisello Balsamo, Milan: San Paolo, 1996), 604–5.

[7]   Ibid.

formula: "There is no God but God and Muhammad is His Messenger." Their religious practices consist in prayer, almsgiving, fasting, pilgrimage, and holy war. The latter is understood as the effort to affirm the rights of God in all settings of life and demands above all spiritual combat to conform oneself to the divine will, and therefore the missionary effort to extend Islam (this submission) — if need be, through armed conquest. Today, Western civilization, secularized, individualistic, and consumeristic, is penetrating the Islamic world and corroding it from within, arousing reactions by Islamic fundamentalists that have led them to an aversion toward Christianity.

Is it not better to engage in dialogue than to foment division and fight each other?

The Magisterium of the Church continuously recommends that, in their encounters with members of other religions, Christians should profess without ambiguity their Christian Faith. With this indispensable condition and the principle of authentic religious freedom as our starting point, the Church encourages Christians to act with great charity and dialogue toward all. It is necessary that we live our Christian Faith without judgments and adversity.

Does the Catholic Church continue to be tolerant and charitable today?

The fact that John Paul II knew from firsthand experience the obtuseness of all types of ideologies, and their inability to recognize their own errors, led him to express forcefully the truth that sets us free in his strong passion for the truth, greater than any worldly calculation or any prudential measure.

The act of courage and occasion for dialogue on the pope's part brought about a transformation that was made concrete on March 12, 2000, during the central event of the Day of Purification of Memory and Pardon,[8] during which he asked forgiveness for the sins committed in the service of the truth (intolerance for dissidents, wars of religion, oppression during the Crusades, the Inquisition); that divided the unity of the Body of Christ (excommunications, persecutions, schisms); against Israel, the people of the First Covenant (contempt, acts of hostility, silence); against love, peace, peoples, cultures, and other religions (committed during evangelization); against human dignity and the unity of the human race (toward women, races, ethnic groups); against the fundamental rights of the person (the last, the poor, the unborn, economic and social injustices, marginalization); and for the evils of our day (atheism, religious indifference, ethical relativism, the violation of the right to life, indifference to the poor).[9]

8   After the pope's intervention that year, January 27 has continued to be celebrated in Italy as the Day of Remembrance, marking the day when troops of the Red Army entered Auschwitz in 1945, a memorial "with the aim of remembering the Shoah … the racial laws, the Italian persecution of Jewish citizens, and the Italians who suffered deportation, imprisonment, death, as well as those who, in various fields and walks of life, opposed the project of extermination, and who, risking their own lives, saved others and protected the persecuted" (law n. 211, of July 20, 2000). After UN Resolution 60/7 was passed on November 1, 2005, the Day of Remembrance became an international celebration among all member states every January 27, in commemoration of the victims of Nazism, the Holocaust, and of all who protected the Jews.

9   This is the list of John Paul II's "apologies." Aware that "faith has nothing to fear before historical research because the truth has its source in God" and that "recognizing the faults of the past serves to reawaken our consciences before the compromises of the present," Karol Wojtyła pronounced the "*mea culpa*" of the Church for the divisions among Christian churches (1980), the participation of Christians in wars (1983), the lack of a response to the appeal of the reformer Luther (1983), the incomprehension of Calvin and Zwingli (1984), conflicts with our "Muslim brothers" (1985), antisemitism (1986), the extermination of the Australian Aborigines (1986), failing to denounce social injustices (1988), religious fundamentalism (1988), the condemnation of Jan Hus (1990), the Great Schism with the Orthodox Church (1991), inaction during the Holocaust (1991), the abuses committed

But shouldn't those who have been intolerant be the first to ask forgiveness? What does John Paul II have to do with this?

The attention of public opinion displayed the extraordinary importance of the act of asking forgiveness, so tenaciously desired by John Paul II, overcoming fierce internal resistance (as if it were a matter of an act of personal piety on behalf of John Paul II, and not the object of a solemn document such as an encyclical).

The pope clarified, among other things, that for the Church, "This request for pardon must not be understood as an expression of false humility or as a denial of her two-thousand-year history, which is certainly richly deserving in the areas of charity, culture and holiness. Instead she responds to a necessary requirement of the truth, which, in addition to the positive aspects, recognizes the human limitations and weaknesses of the various generations of Christ's disciples."[10]

Can poor religious formation lead to rebellion, transgression, and thus atheism?

Due to the limits of human reason with respect to the divine mind, and due to the depth of the infinite and absolute value of God, we can

---

against Native Americans (1992), the slave trade carried out by Christians (1992), the errors committed in the Galileo case (1994), acquiescence to dictatorships (1994), the errors of the Inquisition (1994), the responsibility of Catholics in the genocide in Rwanda (1994), offenses against the dignity of women (1995), the Crusades (1995), the Second World War, carried out in a Christian civilization (1995), the wars of religion (1995), the complicity of Christians with the mafia (1995), the errors of the popes throughout history (1995), the faults of Christians in the persecution of the Jews (2000), and the atrocities committed by Catholics in Bosnia Herzegovina (2003). For an in-depth look at the subject, see Antonio Mastantuono, *The Foreign Prophecy: Forgiveness in Several Figures of Contemporary Philosophy*, (Cinisello Balsamo, Milan: San Paolo, 2002).

10 Discourse given September 1, 1999.

know him only as in a mirror dimly, as St. Paul says. Consequently, we have a limited comprehension of God, and we can easily suffer from poor religious information and formation.

There is in fact a very precise formulation of our relationship with God, the fruit of divine revelation and of Christian witness. During our years of catechism, we were instructed about God with this formulation, taking it very seriously. In it, God was proposed in sharp definition. We learned that God *must be* known and loved thanks to our intelligence and our efforts. We gave it our best: because God is God, because God is Absolute, because it is unimaginable not to accept God.

Many, however, remained distant from God throughout their adolescence due to that particular formulation of Him. Perhaps it reduced Him to a mere veneer of rituality and nothing more.

For some time, they were convinced that the distance was because they were not good enough or spiritual enough, or else not open enough to the love of God. Then, as life moved on, God was perceived as being ever farther away: He went His way and we went ours. The image of a cold and authoritarian Eternal Father remained impressed on them.

Well, this was the image of a God who neither loves nor frees His creatures. It took only a single stone to shatter the entire foundation of clay, bringing the whole statue to ruin.

Often, the instinct to place blame arises — on our catechists, parents, or certain parish priests, for example. But in reality, the fault is not theirs. The issue lies in the formulation itself, and more fundamentally, it is no one's fault at all, for understanding God is not something achieved in an instant. On the contrary, every path to God is imperfect — both because God is God and because man perceives Him according to his own limitations.

There are many conceptions of God: those of philosophers, artists, poets, theologians, scientists, and astronomers, as well as those found in natural religions. But, as I said, they remain conceptions.

For some, overcoming the "crisis of religious education" proves especially difficult. Either they have entrusted themselves directly to the Father, recalibrating and integrating their understanding, or they have become rigid, clinging intolerantly to the formulation they were given. As a result, as I said, the latter remain alone and distant, consumed by anger, sadness, and atheism.

To what extent can "tepid" or "fundamentalist" Christians do harm?

Every adult ought to be capable of taking responsibility for his choices. Immature and impressionable personalities, however, struggle to decide and commit.

The believer who is neither hot nor cold — a Christian in theory but not in practice — can undoubtedly have a negative influence. Mahatma Gandhi maintained that "actions count. Our thoughts, however good they might be, are imitation pearls until they are transformed into actions. Be the transformation that you desire to see happen in the world!"

One senses, then, a certain weariness among some of the faithful when it comes to bearing witness, upholding the good, and resisting evil. In the fifth canto of *Paradiso*, Beatrice explains to Dante how Christians take their commitments to God too lightly and urges them to be more steadfast:

> Christians, proceed with greater gravity: do not be like a
> feather at each wind, nor think that all immersions wash
> you clean. You have both Testaments, the Old and New,
> you have the shepherd of the Church to guide you; you

need no more than this for your salvation. If evil greed would summon you elsewhere, be men, and not like sheep gone mad.... Do not act like the foolish, wanton lamb that leaves its mother's milk. (*Paradiso* 5:73ff)

The inconsistency of some Christians is a catastrophe, leading the "weak" to long for the greener grass on the other side — to rebel, transgress, reject the Faith, and fall prey to all manner of devilish deception.

If a priest's sole objective is to chase after those who have strayed, seeking only to bring them back to the religiosity of former times, I consider his aims misguided. In certain ecclesiastical contexts, religiosity is so overemphasized that it provokes rejection. In my view, we need to engage with those outside the Faith and receive from them what might be called "the added value of the profane" — the insights they have gained from their experience beyond the "sacred paddock." Just as the painful reality of having abandoned the Faith can ultimately purify and rekindle belief in those who return, so too can this "added value" offer something to those who have remained within.

What can you say about the "Christian" God?

The Son of God, Jesus Christ, and Christianity do not constitute a religion in the sense of natural or institutionalized religions; nor are they merely a philosophy, made up of doctrines, truths, and speculative treatises; nor a moral system concerned primarily with its own perpetuation. Jesus Christ, the God-Man, is a person, an event — one that unveils unheard-of perspectives on the identity of God, as well as on human values, vocation, and destiny. In Christ crucified, God's concrete love for humanity is fully revealed. "The Crucified One is not a man who died for God, but the Son of God who dies for man."[11]

---

[11] Bruno Maggioni, *The Our Father* (Milan: Life and Thought, 1995), 25.

In the experience of faith in Jesus Christ, one makes an entirely different reading of God, therefore. Christianity comes to the clear experience and affirmation of the unicity of God and of His transcendence, an affirmation already contained in the Jewish tradition. Thus, the singularity of Christianity consists in having discovered the *self-identification* and *self-revelation* of God as *Father and Son and Holy Spirit.*

The revolutionary scope of Christianity is not only in having assumed on the level of values the "transcendent" and the "sacred," but of having given back dignity and autonomy to the "profane."

Thanks to its constant attention to "creation," to the "incarnation" and "redemption," Christian experience and culture enlarged immensely the area of the sacred, to the point of making it coincide with "everything created by God" and, in particular, with every human being, of whom even one is worth "much more than many sparrows," according to the Gospel.

The Christian lives his relationship with God in a gratifying experience of adoration "in spirit and truth." He encounters God always and everywhere, beyond any spatial-temporal limitations, because God manifests Himself in man's actions, in creation, in history no less than in religious rites celebrated within a temple.

Fr. Gabriele's loving relationship with Don Giacomo Alberione (1884–1971), founder of the Congregation to which the well-known exorcist belongs.

CHAPTER TWO

The Restoration of the Icon

"We are pierced through, and must be pierced through, by the atrocious doubt of having truly comprehended what we say about God, or of having exchanged God for an idol of our own fabrication, though not of stone or gold, but of human ideas, and of hopes that are human, all too human, with frivolous consolations and empty chatter."[12]

Fr. Gabriele, the good exists, does it not?

Mythology, religion, ethics, philosophy, all widely discuss good and evil. The presence and the power of good and evil result in one excluding the other, without any possibility of compromise. Absolutely, the good exists, of course! In our own time as well as ever. It does not always appear, however, nor is it publicized. What is propagated, however, is what today is called *euphobia*, the rejection of the good.

If good did not exist and if we were not capable of doing good, we would no longer be human beings.

Your books on the devil have sold widely; do you think this one about God will have the same popularity?

This one on Our Lord is good news, and it will therefore be mostly ignored. The ones about the devil are bad news and are quite popular for that very reason.

---

[12] Karl Rahner, *The Figure of the Modern Priest* (Rome: Pauline Editions, 1969), 22–23.

I hope this book will find its way into the daily news, precisely because it offers a corrective to the attitude of highlighting exclusively the negative.

It is often said in journalistic circles that good news doesn't make the headlines. Yet if an act of love is far more significant and captivating than a gesture of hatred, why, then, does it struggle to find legitimate and frequent space in the pages of newspapers?

To prevent the news from fueling a defense of evil and delinquency, it is at least reduced to a summary form, framed in dispassionate terms, with a denunciatory tone, restraint, and essentiality.

Imagine we are sailing along the placid waters of a river while listening to *On the Blue Danube* by Johann Strauss or *The Moldau* by Bedřich Smetana — compositions marked by a serene, flowing rhythm, though at times surging with intensity. I compare the pleasure of such delights to the experience of a fortunate man who, even in adversity, remains in calm waters, savoring the many fruits of a joyful life — benefits received, lived, and shared. As long as he continues along this river, he delights in the good and does not allow himself to be shaken by evil but rather stands firm in resisting it.

It is unfortunate, then, that the "experts in the good" either keep themselves hidden or are entirely ignored. This is no small problem, for without such figures, we lack the reference points that could make the good appealing, something to be savored and widely known — capable of drawing in those who are distracted or vulnerable to evil.

To arouse this attraction, is it not more useful to speak about the good rather than be interested in evil and the devil, as you do in your ministry as an exorcist?

The topic under discussion is not always of our own choosing. If it's raining, we cannot help but say it's raining; and so we go about opening our umbrella to stay dry. If attention is given to Satan, it means he is present and active as well. We cannot just ignore him.

Thus, I took up this subject. If there's a hailstorm, I have to think about hail.

You have been consulted, called, and interviewed quite often on television and by journalists. Are you not suspicious that someone might try to exploit you?

I am not inclined to see the devil everywhere. It seems that those who consult me ask for clarifications or whatever concerning my ministry in good conscience and faith. I respond and tell them what I think, based on my experience as an exorcist and referring to the demonology studied and documented by Holy Church. Are they trying to lure me into a trap? The evil one is not always successful; I don't think they are either. I approach everyone with simplicity, but also with firmness and determination, because I think I'm on the side of the Strong One, namely that of Our Lord.

What terms do you use in talking about good and evil?

Christianity *personifies* and *identifies* the good with God and the angels. In fact, God is the *highest good*. Evil is identified with the devil, who incarnates it and personifies it.

Do people know that God personifies the highest good?

First of all, God knows better than anyone that people are not satisfied with merely an idea of Him; they seek His presence — the truest love, authentic and available. People are often deceived, disillusioned, angry, and unhappy, and for this reason, they continue searching for God, for Eden, for discernment, and for the knowledge of good and evil in their lives.

Most people are attuned to reality and concreteness. When confronted with lofty theology and spirituality, they often find it burdensome or unrelatable. They expect the Good God to be near them, just around the corner — not a mere abstraction. Pope Francis speaks of God in a way that is concrete, simple, and deeply moving.

At heart, I would say, people understand that God is the highest good; yet they long to encounter Him here and now.

What would you say about those who proclaim a "faded" God?

They would do well to reflect on their lives, to seriously examine their experience and understanding of God. Otherwise, they risk becoming an obstacle. Mary Magdalene, Peter, Paul, and the other apostles *saw* Him as He rolled away the stone from the tomb of their hearts, granting them new life and bringing them peace. For this reason, certain "missionaries" who neglect such an examination of conscience should no longer stand in the space between the individual and God. They should step aside.

In your estimation, do you consider it urgent for the Catholic Church to revise its concept and understanding of God?

Not merely my opinion, but a long-established reality: The Church has been engaged in this process since its very foundation. I refer here to the first great revisionist — Saul, later the Apostle Paul — who was compelled to radically "reconsider" his understanding of God.

He was on his way to Damascus, intent on actively opposing the name of Jesus and hunting down Christians. As a zealous adherent of the strictest sect of the Jewish religion, he saw it as his duty to fulfill the Mosaic Law, "seething with threats and bloodshed against the

Lord's disciples," arresting them, imprisoning them, forcing them to blaspheme, and vowing to condemn them to death.

"As I made my journey and drew near to Damascus, about noon a great light from heaven suddenly shone about me. And I fell to the ground and heard a voice saying to me, 'Saul, Saul, why do you persecute me?' And I answered, 'Who are you, Lord?' And he said to me, 'I am Jesus of Nazareth, whom you are persecuting'" (Acts 22:6–8).

Blinded by the brilliance of Christ's radiance, Saul's vessel of wrath was shattered — only to be remade into a chalice of divine election and grace.

This providential upheaval buried once and for all Saul's presumption of possessing the truth about God and imposing it by the sword. Poor God — and, above all, poor Saul — though he landed on his feet! The waters of Baptism cleansed him of the blood he had shed in the name of the God of his fathers, a God who, in Paul's transformation, passed from his mind into his heart. He withdrew into the Arabian desert to acquire perfect knowledge of the risen Lord and to grasp his message of God's paternity and maternity.

Before his conversion, Saul and God were like a wing wedged into the crevices of the rocks. The revealed Word was read and communicated in corrupted letters — devoid of paternal tenderness and filial joy, lacking fire and light. But in Christ, Paul was remade. Stripped of intolerance, he was clothed in Christ. His thoughts ascended from the ruins of a narrow and merciless understanding of God — one bound to the mere letter of the Law — toward the living revelation inscribed in the Spirit.

As he passed through the breeze of his three years of preaching in Arabia, he "reread" and "rearranged" himself in Christ, who in turn "redesigned" the face of the Father, illuminating it as a divine free gift, transforming it from mere bread into flesh, from wine into blood.

The recognition of limits and the emptiness of certain rigid impositions can purify the conscience of its distortions, reordering it in the clarity of contemplation and the love that gives itself freely. This transformation allowed Paul to proclaim Our Lord no longer *"in a distorted way."* To do otherwise would be to perpetuate, in our own time, the already-proclaimed "death" of both God and man.

The proclamation of the marvelous works of God and of man remains credible only when it is first lived in the interior life, within the existential realm of the soul. From there, it can then be made public — even on television — and in ways that astonish the world.

Will we priests be capable of witnessing to the true God?

More than anyone else, we priests must speak about God, bear witness to Him, and propose Him to the people as their greatest good. There was no need for Celentano to encourage us to do so at the San Remo Music Festival in 2012.

If we confuse His identity, we mislead the people from understanding the truth about God. St. Paul, writing to the Christians in Rome concerning the leaders who must "instruct others" about God, explicitly and clearly condemns those leaders when they fail to do so. Reconsidering several criticisms of the ancient Scriptures in this regard, he warns that "the name of God is blasphemed among the gentiles due to them." Thus, as the renowned theologian Karl Rahner held, "We are pierced through, and must be pierced through, by the atrocious doubt of having truly comprehended what we say about God, or of having exchanged God for an idol of our own fabrication, though not of stone or gold, but of human ideas, and of hopes that are human, all too human, with frivolous consolations and empty chatter."[13]

---

[13] Ibid.

What are the conditions for comprehending, witnessing, and proclaiming the true God?

Every human being believes he is proclaiming God because he considers himself properly informed, an expert in the matter. Yet thinking in this way, he will certainly not resolve the profound problem of God, of evil, or of suffering in the world — though he may find some personal comfort in the attempt.

It is not right for us priests to presume an exclusive right to proclaim God, placing obstacles and preventing others from doing so alongside us. In truth, it is the Savior — not men — who decides when and to whom He wishes to reveal Himself.

We begin to understand that God is truly God when we recognize that we do not know Him as well as we ought. We must simply wait, with the expectation of coming to know Him more fully — what, in Christian language and experience, is called hope, expectancy. And this attitude, believe me, is no small matter.

Why shouldn't the faithful accompany us in understanding and in testifying to Our Lord?

Fr. Gabriele, how do the faithful live their relationship with God?

Today, we often find ourselves before individuals who are deeply unsettled yet ask few questions. It is essential to invite them to seek profound answers, to have an authentic experience of God — one that reveals Him as credible and trustworthy.

Many people live their relationship with God as that of a servant to a master, unfamiliar as they are with divine benevolence. They see Him as a despot to be resisted, someone against whom they must rebel and transgress. As long as they continue to experience God merely as the Almighty and not as a *Papa*, their relationship with Him deteriorates into a broken dialogue.

Neither natural religiosity nor structured religious practice has eliminated the distance between humanity and God. The primordial attitude of fear, submission, and indifference persists, as described in Scripture: *"I heard the sound of thee in the garden, and I was afraid, because I was naked; and I hid myself"* (Gen. 3:10).

As is well known, religious people often turn to God seeking healing, offering Him gifts, making supplications, purifying their conscience, and performing good deeds — all in hopes of receiving what they have asked for, such as the salvation of their soul. But if the infirm are not made whole, it is God who is seen to have failed. This leads to doubt — either in His existence or in His goodness and generosity.

It is not enough to be religious and devout, though we owe due respect to those who taught us religion and devotion. Our parents, teachers, faithful parish priests, and catechists passed on to us what they themselves had experienced and understood about God. But that alone is not sufficient to have a truly fulfilling encounter with God the Father, Son, and Holy Spirit.

What can you say about the true God?

It seems it is not reasonable or even permissible to present Our Lord as a sad failure, a weakened metaphysical type, an old, suspicious tyrant as he was described, for example, by the young Sigmund Freud.

Let us try to "imagine Him" first of all from the standpoint of human beings without religion, lacking ideological biases, just as it comes from our body and soul. In a way that renders Him comprehensible to simple people, not particularly religious or especially advanced. Pope Francis is a true master in this.

It is clear that God the Father, revealed in Jesus Christ, is neither ugly nor nasty. He did not behave that way with the fratricidal Cain or with the traitor Judas, and not even with the devil.

Who is God, then?

From the perspective of our creaturehood, we can understand God's identity and nature as *Being, Fullness, Love.* He lacks nothing and asks for nothing for Himself, for if He did, He would not be God. In Himself and for us, He is the fullness of life, goodness, and love — an overflowing wellspring that loves and creates.

We, by nature, are defined by need; God, by nature, is gift. Ours is the cup; His is the fountain. He is fulfilled in loving and in love — this is His very reason for being. Divine happiness consists in being Love and in giving freely, long before human beings ever recognize the gift or seek to merit it.

What do you mean by a simple human being?

Need, at its core, defines the identity and nature of the real human being. As creatures, we are dependent on everything. To exist and to live, we seek life, food, health, work, education, culture, love, freedom, the experience of God, and eternity. From the moment of birth, we *cry out* our need, instinctively reaching for our mother's breast.

The good — our personal Eden — lies above all in eating, drinking, sleeping, keeping warm, laughing, and feeling accepted and loved. If we are happy, good, and unharmed, it is because we have received these essential gifts from the very start. If, however, we are deprived of them, we become dissatisfied, sorrowful, and even aggressive.

Who responds to our needs?

Our parents, families, schools, and society respond to our requests with all their services. Once we are adults, we continue to need everything, but we mostly procure it for ourselves through our own means. If we need bread, we buy it from the bakery; if we need medicine, we buy it in a pharmacy. Affection cannot be bought, however; to have it we turn to those dear to us.

Is it always possible to find satisfaction?

There are those who have lived the pain of not having been accepted, loved, nourished. Many years ago, I saw this pain written in a book: "I just wanted my father to hug me and to tell me he would never have abandoned me, that he would remain near me to protect me from everyone."[14] This is a wound that is not easily healed because the person has been robbed of something that was their *due*, something extremely vital. Parents, on the other hand, give what they have and are.

To whom can one turn when one finds no satisfaction?

Don't tell me to turn exclusively to science, psychology, anthropology, war, medicine, the economy, or politics — for despite possessing all these, countless human beings still die from ignorance, hunger, illness, and violence.

Don't tell me to turn to freedom alone. Today's fanatical obsession with the right to freedom and free thought, without the necessary education and formation in its responsible and fruitful use, leaves individuals, communities, and the entire world disoriented. The abuse of freedom fuels sects, conspiracies, armed conflicts, and every kind of evil, further alienating humanity from itself and from its divine Creator.

Everyone — individuals, families, schools, governments, and the Church — must ensure that the fundamental needs of all are met so that every person may live, for no one enters the world by choice.

---

[14] Lara Cardella, *I Wanted the Trousers* (Milan: Mondadori, 1989), 73.

The suffering that comes from lacking essential goods has the power to pierce the heavens and turn into a plea: "Give us this day our daily bread" — in other words, the *necessary*, the *indispensable* good. And it is inhumane to turn to heaven in supplication when human and material resources already exist that could provide for all.

Can you say more about the sacrality of the human being?

"Sacralized" religion is, by definition, that which is already deemed sacred and, as a result, separates itself from the profane — that which is considered *not* sacred. Let me explain.

We must recognize that we are sacred simply by virtue of being *human*. This is because we possess an *innate and essential need for God*, seeking in Him the *natural* and *definitive* answer to our fundamental needs — needs that, alone or even collectively, we cannot fully satisfy.

It is in the lived experience and awareness of being *sacred* that the individual rediscovers both his value and his limits, even before professing any religious creed or adhering to its imperatives and observances.

The original sacred identity of man and woman must be remembered, acknowledged, celebrated, reaffirmed, and articulated as an archetypal reality, common to every human being. Once one attains this awareness, the movement toward God becomes *natural* — toward the God who loves, designs, and creates the human being *in His image and likeness.* Seen in this way, we are already "something very good," inherently sacred, without requiring initiation, sacralization, or the added values of religious rites and rituals.

Christianity affirms this intrinsic sacrality, safeguarded in every human being as if in a vault, recognizing that no crime or sin can strip a person of it. So much so that Jesus Christ, "the only Son of God, who is in the bosom of the Father" (John 1:18), became man, died, and rose again to guarantee this reality for all. The religious dimension does not *add* to this sacrality; rather, it *recognizes* and *celebrates* the union of the sacred and the divine.

Is it possible to have an experience of God as the Son revealed Him in the bosom of the Father?

Throughout the history of religions, God has not always been presented in a true and unambiguous way. More often than not, He has been depicted as an authoritarian deity — demanding, yet somehow needy, requiring something from human beings. If, for this reason, humanity has not yet lived its experience of God in a state of *happiness*, it suggests that religion, the priesthood, proclamation, catechesis, spirituality, devotion, ritual, witness, and even exorcism remain merely expedients — still inadequate and lacking.

I am not pointing fingers at anyone, but the fact remains: despite the best intentions, neither humanity nor the world has truly grasped God. Some have certainly succeeded, but not all. Given the state of the world today, it is evident that we have yet to encounter the *loving* God in a profound and universal way — nor are we likely to do so anytime soon. This, of course, does not mean that He does not exist.

What must we do: Roll up our sleeves and get to work?

Let us try to salvage the best of natural religion and of the world religions. However, it is indispensable that we become aware of our limits, our poverty, our aspirations, and our requests, but also of the potential and sacrality we have in such great abundance.

Is that really how things are between human beings and God?

Man and God are not "abridged" editions — simple realities that can be neatly summarized — but rather values of unfathomable depth. No matter how great our intelligence, we cannot reduce them to our paradigms, projects, undertakings, religions, crusades, or holy wars. What has been said about the human being is confirmed by experience; what concerns the existence and identity of God, however, is inferred from the deep longing within us — an interior openness to Him — precisely because He alone fills the existential void of our profoundly needy nature.

Thirst would be meaningless if there were no water to quench it.

Yet, speaking of man and of God is no simple task. The experience of evil could seem to disqualify both. The world and humanity do not resemble God, nor do they reflect Him, for they are often merciless, immoral, and unkind. For the human spirit, it is difficult to perceive the imprint of divine tenderness in such a reality.

Hatred arises from our lack of fulfillment. When we seek the definitive satisfaction of our needs and our inner emptiness in other creatures, we receive only human answers — if we receive them at all. And these answers never fully satisfy, for no human being is the fullness of life, goodness, and love.

Thus, instead of extending compassion and solidarity to our fellow human beings, joining them in the same boat to reach the harbor of the good, we turn against them in frustration. It is our *malaise* that makes us bitter. Some declare themselves atheists, but they are not so much angry with God as they are with those who distort our understanding of Him and misrepresent His message.

How can we continue to restore the icon of the human being and of God?

We must first be convinced that at the heart of the universe and humanity is *us* — each one of us, who is a part of it. The world and humanity are like a field: I am the field worker.

I can fill this field with the abundance of a fulfilled heart, or I can sow it with curses born of existential pain. But wounds must not remain open indefinitely. Life must be given meaning with realism, healed by nourishing it with goodness.

And do not tell me, in all honesty, that you cannot distinguish between good and evil.

When we turn to God, we are certain of standing on the side of goodness and of finding true fulfillment.

To think of ourselves and of God in this way means aligning ourselves with reality — keeping our feet on the ground, seeking where we may truly receive, playing our part well, and allowing God to play His.

Fr. Amorth with the Passionist Father Candido Diamantini,
who launched him in his ministry as an exorcist.

CHAPTER THREE

The Pail and the Sea

"The pail said to the little boy: 'Throw me into the sea and I'll drink it all!' He let it sink to the bottom. 'Pull me out, it's too much.' He fished it out and filled with as much as he needed."[15]

How does God manifest Himself?

Our Lord's desire is to communicate and share His infinite goodness and love — something He absolutely cannot keep to Himself.

There are many paths, instruments, and people through whom He reveals Himself.

Sacred Scripture is one such means — a dialogue between God and humanity. The Bible serves as the historical memory of God's presence, words, and works within the unfolding of human events. It reveals His presence not as something external but as intimately woven into both the extraordinary and the ordinary moments of daily life, manifesting within historical, social, domestic, and personal circumstances alike.

Would we truly die if we were to encounter and see God?

God is like the vast sea — impossible to contain within the limits of a mere pail. If, however, Our Lord were to reveal Himself to us *entirely* in this life, we would be so irresistibly drawn to Him that we would

[15]   Angelo De Simone, "The Pail and the Sea," in *Reed Flute. Poems*, unpublished.

lose all taste for this world, desiring only to return to Him and remain there forever.

This, for example, was the experience of St. Joseph of Cupertino, of whom it was said: *vulann, vulann, s'nn jett 'mParavis* (flying, flying, he left for paradise). Try saying it in your fine Neapolitan dialect!

God manifests Himself to humanity gradually, *dosing* our happiness in a way that is always proportionate to the recipient. He slowly conforms the soul to the overwhelming power of divine love, which is revealed in an incarnate manner through the Son made man — so that it may be savored even more fully in the perfect joy of blessed eternity.

How does Sacred Scripture begin?

Opening the great book of the Bible, we find in its first chapters the account of the origin of the universe and humanity, as well as the sin of our first parents and their children.

The biblical writers describe how God makes His plan of love known to all humanity. Not only does He descend to the level of human beings, becoming present among them as their Creator, but He also engages in personal dialogue with those He has called.

He reveals Himself in His covenant with the patriarch Abraham, in His struggle with Jacob at the river Jabbok, in the liberation of His people from Egypt, in the crossing of the Red Sea and the Jordan River, in the covenant at Sinai, and later, through the repentance of David, the vision of the prophet Elijah on Horeb, and the sufferings and ultimate redemption of the Servant of Yahweh.

Abraham, in particular, represents the humanity God has blessed and gathered into a land that serves as a new paradise. The supreme gifts of land, descendants, and blessings are freely given by God to the patriarch, even though Abraham attempts to secure them by his own means or through his tribe.

The patriarchs — Abraham, Jacob, and Joseph — struggle to accept the divine gift, which had been unknown to them before. Yet, they come to understand that, having been chosen as mediators between God and the people, they do not stand in God's place; rather, they have been chosen within salvation history to carry His name to *all* humanity.

Through these and countless other callings and events, God's love and power are revealed — along with His willingness to humble Himself and share in the exile and suffering of humanity throughout the course of history.

How is this to be interpreted?

The divine author called certain individuals to speak of Him, and from their words, the living tradition of an entire people was formed. Over time, this tradition was enriched, and later, it was committed to writing — at times in response to the pressing needs of the moment. The divine Spirit illuminated and guided the minds of those who proclaimed these teachings and set them down in writing, adapting Himself to their ways of hearing, expressing, narrating, and composing.

Thus, for example, He speaks both through the refined style of the prophet Isaiah and the passionate intensity of the prophet Jeremiah, though their styles are so markedly different.

God communicates in a human manner to the sacred writers, working through the conditions of their time, their culture, their languages, and the literary forms they employed — whether historical, prophetic, poetic, sapiential, or other modes of expression.

Yet, while considering these human aspects, Sacred Scripture must ultimately be interpreted with the guidance of the Spirit of God, through whom it was written. For this reason, one must carefully attend to both the content and the unity of all of Scripture.

One who reads the Scared Scriptures cannot fail to be struck by the violence it portrays: How can violence in the Bible be justified, when it was inspired by God?

Many detect in the Bible the violent and destructive potential inherent in every religion. For this reason, they tend to ignore entire sections of this book, marked as it is by violent narratives. The heretic Marcion, according to St. Ireneus's testimony, even thought that "the God whom the Law and the Prophets proclaimed was malicious and warlike."

In reality, Sacred Scripture speaks not only of life and the good but also of evil, violence, and the evil one, who is their source and cause. It does so without omitting any aspect of life or death, embracing the full scope of human existence, which is not always a peacefully flowing river. The inclusion of violent events serves to highlight a history worn thin by its distance from goodness and from God. At the same time, it reveals the surpassing power of goodness and awakens within us a loving attraction toward God, our highest good.

To use an analogy, there is the story of the nun Roswitha, born in 936. She had an exceptional mental vivacity, without precedent in the Middle Ages for a woman and a nun. This writer, so ahead of her time, had to bend her will, as she herself documents, "to describe the deplorable follies of souls abandoned to forbidden loves," so as to be able "to exalt ... the glory of innocent souls; because just as the sweet words of lovers are capable of seducing, so all the higher the glory of divine assistance and more splendid is the merit of those who triumph."[16]

The Bible, and I am not mistaken here, has recourse to this same expedient.

---

[16] Umberto Albini and Gianna Petrone, *History of Theater*, vol. 2, "From the Roman Empire to Humanism" (Milan: Garzanti, 1982), 82.

Thus, the reader of Sacred Scripture cultivates a wisdom that has its feet planted on the ground. Such realism, the key to reading the holy book, allows one to avoid the path of violence toward self and others. If he were to become violent and nauseated by it, he would be enticed to abandon the pathway of unhappiness for self and others. So he heads down the narrow path that leads to God, to the good and to happiness; he becomes accustomed to the "light yoke" of the "perfect joy" that the world is incapable of providing.

Is this how we discover divine teaching?

Since religious man longs to ascend to God but cannot do so on his own, God Himself takes the initiative to draw near to him. As Scripture teaches, after choosing *His* people, God educates them — first through the natural law, which applies to all humanity, and then in a special way through a positive legislative structure.

Through those He calls, God establishes moral and juridical norms, along with cultic and ritual ordinances. At the heart of these stands the Decalogue — the Ten Commandments — given as an imperative by God Himself. The various names attributed to the law (*teaching, testimony, precept, commandment, decision, judgment, word, will, path of God*) indicate that it transcends the limitations of human legislation.

The priests serve as the custodians of God's law, teaching it within the sanctuary to uphold both worship and fidelity to the Lord. Israel's historians and sages exalt the law, while the psalmists celebrate its greatness, expressing their love for it and embracing it as "a lamp for their feet and a light for their path." The prophets, however, chastise priests, kings, and the people when they neglect the law. In prophetic literature especially, the law is infused with a profound spiritual dimension — not merely commandments inscribed on stone tablets, but divine imperatives etched into human hearts.

Israel's devotion to the divine law intensifies particularly in times of crisis — natural disasters, epidemics, famines, exile, and sieges by foreign pagan powers, as in the era of the Maccabees. When national and communal life is restored, the first priority is always the renewal of fidelity to God and observance of His law — only afterward do they rebuild the temple and the walls of Jerusalem.

The law transmitted by God — through Moses, for example — also takes on a strongly authoritative and juridical character, as it serves to establish Israel as a distinct and ordered nation. Once this formation is complete, however, God gradually reveals Himself to them not merely as Lawgiver but as *Shepherd, Father,* and *Mother.*

Even today, the Jewish people recognize the divine law as the supreme rule of life, though its interpretation has, over time, been fragmented by various schools of thought into an intricate web of precepts, prohibitions, and burdensome regulations. When the *soul* of the divine law is lost, it becomes an oppressive yoke — one that, paradoxically, religious radicalism seeks to impose on all.

What lies behind the Ten Commandments?

Binding together pages of historical events, sentiments and poetry, wisdom, and life in God, Sacred Scripture clearly reveals that behind the Commandments, God the Father is at work. He is deeply moved by the human condition and desires that we savor — not in a conceptual or philosophical manner, but in a total, visceral, and intense way — the experience of His divine presence, truth, and love.

In concrete terms, God the Father assures each of us, "You are the sons of the Lord your God" (Deut. 14:1); "You are my son, today I have begotten you" (Ps. 2:7); "My steadfast love I will keep for him forever" (Ps. 89:28).

And again, Scripture reminds us, "Have we not all one father?" (Mal. 2:10); "Can a mother forget her sucking child, that she should have no compassion on the son of her womb? Even these may forget, yet I will not forget you. Behold, I have graven you on the palms of my hands" (Isa. 49:15–16).

He shares His eternal love with all: "As one whom his mother comforts, so I will comfort you" (Isa. 66:13); like a shepherd who "carries the lambs in his bosom, and gently leads those that are with young" (Isa. 40:11); and again, "Like an eagle that stirs up its nest, that flutters over its young" (Deut. 32:11).

He intervenes in history's most tragic moments, reminding His people, "I loved him, and out of Egypt I called my son! I became to them as one who eases the yoke on their jaws, and I bent down to them and fed them" (Hos. 11:1, 4).

This divine tenderness is expressed in an exquisitely tangible way in the parable of the vineyard (Isa. 5:1–7; 27:2–5) and in the splendid verses of Ezekiel 16:3–14.

Why is it, though, that the vineyard does not correspond to divine love?

The reason can be found in the fact that the demands and prescriptions of the divine law seem harsh and not yet a gift. The vineyard of the Lord, a symbol of humanity and the Lord's beloved people, is incapable of perceiving viscerally the attention and care He has for them. In fact, they do not understand that God has hoed, watered, cleared the stones, cultivated only choice vines, defends it with a tower, has dug a vat, and sent His servants the prophets *only for love*.

What the people experience, on the other hand, is that they are a piece of land that must ensure a harvest for its owner and, if they cannot, they risk remaining a vineyard that is trampled, pulled out, transplanted, and even devastated: demolished and cut down. Israel struggles to have an experience of God as Father and Mother: It is often seen in a state of servitude and subjection before Him;

always in need of reconciliation, liberation, identification, of being loved and blest.

The deepest obstacle to true communion with God remains fear of Him, which prevents a person from experiencing His love as a son.

How can this fear be extinguished?

We must offer the faithful *all the best* that they find in God. There should always be someone to break bread for their spirits. For this reason, the true *apple* that draws men and women — even today — is God Himself, not some alternative to Him, as the *first tempter* deceitfully insinuates.

Goodness, humanity, and God are far more good, beautiful, and attractive than the evil one — this is evident to all who are open to being drawn toward the good. If the faithful were deprived of God the Father, the influence of evil, the devil, and the occult would only grow stronger.

For the most part, the faithful appear weak and disoriented before the evil within them because they do not live in a deep, visceral communion with God as a loving and caring Father.

Should one begin with the commandments, then?

One begins with the *spirit* of the commandments — this is the golden rule for humanity. The spirit of the divine law is superior to the mere letter of the commandments, which must not be observed for their own sake alone.

Nevertheless, God first leads humanity through obedience to the commandments, using them as an instrument through which He continues to speak, educate, discipline, and strengthen His people — so that they may grow into disciplined and mature individuals in every sense.

Thus, the law has a pedagogical function: Those who observe it first experience its weight. Under this burden, they will come to recognize divine love and, in doing so, will long for the Father as sons.

However, if the weight of the law alone prevails and not the love behind it, God will be abandoned by those who remain in a state of spiritual infancy, reacting with tantrums, rebellion, and transgression.

The pedagogy of the law and obedience to the commandments awaken in the soul a longing for and an absolute need for God's free gift. In this way, the servant is transformed into a beloved and blessed son. This new state enables him to embrace the Father's will in love, so that he observes the commandments no longer out of compulsion, but with joy.

The natural law and the Mosaic law serve as instruments — the pedagogical and spiritual path to holiness — through which God communicates with His people and, by extension, with all humanity.

In the Christian life, we see that the son is first guarded and placed under the law, like a child under the care of a tutor or administrator, instructed and disciplined until he reaches maturity in his experience of Christ. This is why St. Paul exhorts the Christians of Thessalonica, still infants in their Faith, to hold fast to the traditions they have received from him.

We must — this is not optional — begin with the commandments. But the golden thread that runs through them and gives them life must always be reaffirmed and renewed: the liberating love of God the Father, justice, mercy, and the free gift of His grace.

Fr. Gabriele presents the Holy Father John Paul II with several copies of the Marian periodical **Mother of God**, *of which he was the director.*

CHAPTER FOUR

Far from the Eyes, Present in the Heart

"If God is for us, who is against us? … Who shall separate us from the love of Christ?"[17]

In which person in particular did God the Father reveal himself?

He communicated with humanity gradually, preparing it step by step to receive the revelation of Himself — a revelation that culminates in Christ: "The Word was with God" and "the only Son, who is in the bosom of the Father," and "the Word became flesh," as we read in the Gospel according to John (1:1, 18, 14). While remaining God, He became the Son of Man — a child, a servant, a laborer subjected to fatigue, poverty, obscurity, silence, hunger, thirst, suffering, and death.

Born a Jew, of a daughter of Israel named Mary, in Bethlehem during the reign of Herod the Great and the Emperor Caesar Augustus, He lived in Nazareth until the age of thirty. He then taught in Palestine for three years and was crucified in Jerusalem under the procurator Pontius Pilate, during the reign of the Emperor Tiberius.

[17]   Romans 8:31, 35.

Why did Jesus address God with the name of Father?

Jesus of Nazareth calls God *Father* because He is not only man but also the Son of God. Both He Himself and His disciples affirm this truth and transmit it through their writings across the ages.

In the Gospels, we read that God Himself proclaims Jesus of Nazareth His "beloved Son." Before His disciples, Jesus "calls God his father," to whom He surrenders Himself "because the Father is with him" and because "the Father loves the Son." On the cross, He remains steadfast in His trust that the Father has not abandoned Him and thus commends His spirit to Him.

Who besides Jesus has had the experience of God the Father?

Jesus invites the disciples to remain with Him, and they are struck by the profound intimacy that unites Him with the Father. The Master tells them that in seeing the Son, they also glimpse the Father, for they dwell within one another and are one. The disciples, too, long to enter into this communion.

Many others have experienced the loving fatherhood of God and communion with the Son — among them, the saints. They encountered God the Father in the events of their lives, drawn and filled by His presence. This deeply fulfilling experience transformed their way of seeing themselves, others, and the world, allowing them to perceive reality with the heart and eyes of the heavenly Father. As a result, they became zealous and tireless workers of goodness, conforming themselves to the person, life, and words of Jesus and His faithful disciples.

Considering all that has been said about the human being and about God, it becomes evident that we are drawn to Him and gratified by His presence because He asks for nothing for Himself. Were

He to do so, He would be needy and no longer the inexhaustible source of all richness.

We are therefore invited to receive Him and allow ourselves to be filled by His *free gift*, which is given both for our joy and for His delight. Our role is simply to allow ourselves to be loved, so that we may, in turn, love Him and our neighbor as ourselves. Without first being filled by Him, it would be like asking a jar to supply water to a fountain or expecting a child to carry his father in his own arms.

God the Father calls each person to communion with Him. He actively seeks out and comes to meet every human being. The first step in this encounter is always His; our response is merely an answer to His *free gift* of love.

The Father reveals Himself gradually and, in doing so, illuminates the person to himself — so that the encounter becomes not only an experience of God but also a revelation of truth, self-knowledge, and a deeper understanding of others.

Communion with God the Father usually takes place in prayer and in listening to His Word: "I will allure her, and bring her into the wilderness, and speak tenderly to her" (Hos. 2:14). From there, we go forth to encounter Him in the least, in the poor, sharing with them the divine *free gift* we have received — one that overflows from within us.

Is it possible to pray in a personal dialogue with God the Father?

Prayer is first of all understanding ourselves, to know who we are; then it is dialogue and communion with the heavenly Father, to know who He is. *To know* does not mean only knowledge of, but *sapere*, tasting and savoring, enjoying and rejoicing to be with ourselves and with God. The habitat of prayer is the *heart*, where the one praying returns to encounter himself in the depths, to decide, to choose, to receive the gift of the Father and share it.

Who can introduce us to prayer?

Jesus of Nazareth often retreated to the mountains or to other remote places to pray, spending at times the entire night in prayer. *Silence* and prayer were constant in the life of Jesus, in particular on the eve of His biggest decisions and in the critical moments of His existence: when He began His mission after His Baptism in the Jordan; when He set off determined toward Jerusalem for the Passover of His death and Resurrection; in the Garden of Gethsemane before His arrest that led Him to the Cross.

Jesus Christ is the praying, itinerant Master. He can teach us how to pray. We too, like the apostles, can ask Him: "Lord, teach us how to pray." The Master not only responds to their requests but asks them to *pray with Him*, to bring about in them trust in God the Father. Thus, He offers the disciples the invitation, " 'Come away by yourselves to a lonely place and rest a while.' For many were coming and going, and they had no leisure even to eat" (Mark 6:31).

How did Jesus express Himself in prayer?

The Gospels document it. Jesus prays in different ways and at different times. In the Gospel of John, the longest of His prayers is reported, addressing the Father: "Father, not my will, but your will be done," because this is His food: "My food is to do the will of Him who sent me and to carry out his work." This is the reason why He came.

In Gethsemane, before His arrest, He counseled the disciples, "My soul is very sorrowful, even to death; remain here and watch," and then confides in the Father, "Abba, Father, all things are possible to thee; remove this cup from me; yet not what I will, but what thou wilt!" His very last prayer is His surrender on the Cross, "Father, into thy hands I commit my spirit!" as St. Luke testifies (23:46).

How should we pray?

Undoubtedly, to learn how to pray, the Son of God is our point of reference. However, we cannot pray as He did or like the saints or like any other person in prayer. When one dialogues with God, Father and Son and Holy Spirit, our prayer is first of all *unique* because it is expressed in an individual and singular form. The space and time of prayer between Our Lord and us cannot be occupied by anyone else.

In a "school of prayer," a teacher might lecture, I might follow a spirituality, utilize a text, have recourse to a formula, but when I dialogue directly with God, Father, Son, and Holy Spirit, *He* is the one who speaks, and I am the one who listens and prays: no one else does this for me.

In communal prayer, such as the eucharistic celebration, we do not gather with the primary intention of "being together," but for being with the Lord crucified and risen, who in turn unites us in a praying assembly. I am not detached from my subjectivity, but I unite it with that of others in the sole intention of receiving the divine free gift.

Furthermore, Jesus invites us to pray "in sprit and in truth" (John 4:23), always and everywhere, without being conditioned by the place or time.

One prays not to make oneself noticed (cf. Matt. 6:5), but to encounter "the Father ... who sees in secret" (Matt. 6:6) of one's heart. And when praying, the Master advises, "do not heap up empty phrases" (Matt. 6:7). Long before Jesus, Kohelet exhorted, "Be not rash with your mouth, nor let your heart be hasty to utter a word before God ... therefore let your words be few" (Eccl. 5:2).

Why is it that when we pray to God the Father, He does not show Himself?

Jesus Christ assured His disciples, "He who has seen me has seen the Father" (John 14:9). In their close contact with the Master, they saw the Father reflected in His incarnate image, accessible to them.

For us in our earthly condition, *we do not have access nor can we see* either God the Father or God the Holy Spirit, as I have said, because He is glorious and resplendent to such a degree that if we were to see Him, we would be totally attracted and no longer free to continue living on this earth.

Can the saying "out of sight, out of mind" be applied to God?

Certainly, but this must not happen. It is *God* above all who *chooses* to be near us. As for us, it is not possible to *keep Him present*, constantly in mind when praying always, because our daily affairs do not allow this.

A continuous vital prayer is possible, however. We ought to paint it in our hearts.

This image leads us to *feel His presence* throughout our entire existence. In fact, we know that we are first *in God's heart*, already in this world, and then we shall contemplate Him in eternal life when our soul will participate in His very essence and divine life.

Can we make an image of God?

We cannot create a faithful image of God, for He is pure spirit.

Yet we ourselves are His *image and likeness* and are therefore sacred — not only by virtue of that identity but also through the good thoughts and sentiments that pass through our minds and hearts and are transformed into actions and good works.

Though simple in His essence, God remains inaccessible, ineffable, incomprehensible, invisible, and unfathomable in this life.

In which other "spaces" can we glimpse God?

When we think of God — the Father, the Son, and the Holy Spirit — it is natural to lift our gaze to the heights, as if He were distant from us, set apart in a *sacred enclosure*, almost in a place of exile.

Yet when we pronounce — or hear — the holy name "Father, Son, and Holy Spirit," we instinctively raise our hand to our forehead, to our chest, and to our shoulders, tracing the sign of the cross.

With this gesture, we express that the Trinity is not outside of us, nor present only in part, but dwells within us completely — from head to foot — loving, accompanying, and sustaining us.

Are we icons of God, then?

Attracted by God, we perform good deeds and are *transformed* into icons of the Trinity, witnesses of Christ crucified and resurrected, voices of the Holy Spirit.

We thus become *signs* of God, but each according in his own measure: crucified to some extent, resurrected to some extent, loved and forgiven, responsibly ready, active, enthusiastic in doing good.

We catch a glimpse of this good even in others, as people and beloved children of God.

How can we come to know Jesus Christ?

We know Jesus Christ through the revelation of the New Testament; in other words, in the Word of God entrusted by Christ the Lord and by the Holy Spirit to the apostles and then to the Church throughout history, as is stated, along with other places, in the conciliar document *Dei Verbum*.

How can we make Jesus Christ the center of the life of the faithful?

First, it is necessary to be with the people and to share their reality, attend to their requests, respond to them by getting involved, recounting our experience of Christ — just as Pope Francis has been doing continuously. Or as St. Paul did, for example: He who gloried in his own righteousness became the executioner of the sons of God, but then placed himself at their disposal and took care of them as a father or a mother nurtures their own children.

How does the attractive power of Jesus Christ transform our spirit?

Our loving Lord descends into our life, our heart, and our actions, he "the fairest of the sons of men" (Ps. 45:2), whose eyes were shrouded by evil men, whose sides were subjected to flogging, whose head was pierced by thorns, whose body was abandoned to insults, the Cross, nails, and death. The "defeat" of the Lord Jesus Christ, persevering in the good and suffering for justice's sake, has a salvific outcome: Through death He reaches life, the wellspring, the table, leading with Himself all humanity, whom He loves to the point of letting Himself be crucified and dying for us.

The human and sacred identity that the Lord Jesus has regained for each of us "by his grace as a gift, through the redemption which is in Christ Jesus" (Rom. 3:24) encourages us to break every tie with evil. In Baptism, in fact, we received as a true divine gift participation in the freedom of Christ, the light that dispels all darkness. In some ways we have been put on a par with the Son, who "went about doing good and healing all that were oppressed by the devil, for God was with him" (Acts 10:38).

Thanks to this autonomy, we are able to participate in His divinity, next to Him and our brethren, through the blessed reception we are given, along with our neighbor and our God. We are no longer timid people, frightened and impressionable by malevolent powers far superior to us. We are free, we are on the side of *the Strong One,* having received from Christ a radical emancipation that renders us serene and trusting because we draw close to Him and are united to Him as our Highest Good. "If God is for us, who is against us?" assures St. Paul. "Who shall separate us from the love of Christ?" (Rom. 8:31, 35).

And this occurs in such a way that the good emanates from within us and may also be found around us, if for no other reason than to contrast evil.

The director of Mother of God *at his desk.*

CHAPTER FIVE

God and Evil

*The good and God himself have no need of
darkness to show that they are light.*

Fr. Gabriele, why is there evil in the world?

We enter into a great mystery. We know that evil surrounds us on all
sides. To this external evil is added the evil within us. Where there is
evil, there is suffering — one of its most unsettling consequences. Even
the *well-off* and the *super-rich* are not spared; they suffer from self-
deception and existential dissatisfaction. Terminal illnesses and the
anguish that accompanies them remain among the most persistent afflictions of humanity, as present today as ever. I will not torment my
mind trying to explain evil or the sharp, unrelenting reality bound to it.

Evil is certainly a mystery, yet you confront it every day.

Before me lies the letter that St. Paul wrote to the Christians in Rome
during his third missionary journey, during the winter he spent in
Greece — a text in which his depiction of evil is strikingly realistic.

The Apostle descends into the abyss of the human condition:
"but they became futile in their thinking and their senseless minds
were darkened. Claiming to be wise, they became fools" (Rom.
1:21–22), engaging in the most reprehensible acts. Yet Paul does not
merely offer an analysis or description of evil; he also presents its
remedy — forgiveness — which reveals the love, mercy, truth, and
justice of the Creator.

Some might argue that evil is necessary for good to shine more brightly, or that deceit must exist for truth to be exalted. But neither goodness nor God Himself requires darkness to prove that they are light.

Ultimately, Paul affirms that evil is committed because the goodness, love, and truth of God are rejected — along with the signs He manifests in nature and in the human heart. Such blindness and rejection lead to wickedness. This happens because someone has cast God in a false light.

When it comes to evil, we must necessarily recognize the work of the angel of darkness, who preaches, again and again, a single message: "God does not love you."

We have come now to the relationship between God and evil, between God and the devil. What is the nature of this relationship?

In one word: the same relationship as between holy water and the devil, as we say.

Did God create the devil and hell?

In the plan of creation, the Son of God stands at the center, Jesus Christ, who is the incarnation of goodness *par excellence*. This is fundamental for understanding the wise and providential plan of God. Thus, everything was made for Christ, with Christ, and in Christ. The Father, loving and contemplating the Son, gave life to invisible realities, among which "the morning star," that is, the angel Lucifer (bearer of light), who then rebelled; as well as the visible realities, among which human beings who, according to Psalm 8, "thou hast made him little less than God" (v. 6). It must be clear, however, that evil, pain, death, hell, and the devil are not the work of God.

I remember one day when the exorcist Fr. Candido Diamantini was expelling a demon. Toward the end of the exorcism, he addressed the evil spirit in these terms: "Get out of here; at any rate, the Lord has prepared a nice warm house for you!" To this the devil replied, "You don't know anything. He [God] was not the one who made hell. We were the ones. He had never thought of such a thing. We have all contributed to it."

What mysterious reason led Lucifer to rebel against God?

Great question! He chose to become evil. How and why he was reduced to such a state is a great mystery, since Lucifer was the best of creatures. Why would he need to rebel against his Creator?

What is our source on the definitive truth about evil and the devil?

First of all, the narrative of the *sin of Adam and Eve* — as well as the role of the tempter — is found in Genesis 3. This account is undoubtedly influenced by the mythological symbolism and religious traditions of northern Mesopotamia from the period of 1800–1500 B.C., which the Jews encountered during their exile in Babylon. Elements such as the tree of life, the envy of a god-serpent, the responsibility of a woman for the loss of primordial happiness, and the flaming sword all have parallels in ancient Mesopotamian traditions.

However, these elements were not simply borrowed wholesale. The editor of the sacred text *purified* them, stripping away the polytheistic, non-historical, and materialistic aspects of that civilization's mythology. They were then integrated into the Jewish wisdom tradition within the framework of salvation history — specifically the paradigm of the Promise and the Covenant with God.

For an accurate interpretation of the text, it is crucial to clarify that while Mesopotamian cosmogony influences the biblical redaction — especially in shared imagery (such as the tree, the forbidden fruit, and the act of illicit plucking) — it is fundamentally distinct in its concept and experience of God. The biblical author acknowledges only *one* God, who reveals Himself as eternal, pre-existent, transcendent, and supreme over all other beings, whether good or evil.

How was evil manifested in the disobedience of Adam and Eve?

Let me begin by saying that in the beginning of the biblical text the sacred writer affirms this about God: "It is not good that man should be alone." He needs "a helper fit for him" (Gen. 2:18). The help God wishes to give him is woman. Thus, the man–woman communion has its origin in God, who desires the complete happiness of both. In creating man and woman, God cancels their respective solitudes, they unite and "become one flesh" (Gen. 2:24). This unity is vital and gratifying such that it ought to equip them for opposing every form of evil and snare, including that of an eventual tempter.

In chapter 3, verses 1–24, the sacred author attempts to explain the first temptation and the first fall of the human couple. The task of probing their behavior and putting them to the test (fidelity or infidelity to the Creator) is entrusted to the *serpent*, considered in the mentality of the time to be a symbol of various divinities, the guardian of their sanctuaries, and the subject of the practice of the dark arts.

The text makes it clear that the tempter does not have a liberating, gratifying, or felicitous experience of the Creator or of man. For this reason, it presents him as hostile and invidious of the prerogatives granted to the man and the woman. He cannot help deceiving them, therefore, presenting them with a good that he himself is not able to acquire, namely being like God. The text does not say, however, that the diabolical initiative was to no avail. He tempts them and they fall, and he savors the "trouble shared is a trouble halved," deceived in thinking he can now remedy the ancient checkmate.

What technique does the tempter make use of?

The understanding between Adam and Eve is quite solid. They have the lively experience and the sure awareness of the divine free gift, of God's effective love. Thus, the tempter aims directly at God in an attempt to disqualify Him in their eyes and separate them from Him. In his discourse he concentrates on the tree of the knowledge of good and evil as well as on the forbidden fruit. Given the restrictions God has placed on them, the diabolical message addressed to both is made very explicit: God is nothing more than a cold legislator. The progenitors have at the same time the perception of the absence of God, since He was strolling about the garden while he was *quite present* and involved with them.

Consequently, they are led to consider themselves *not as God had created them*, namely limited with respect to their Creator. In this way, they could admit to equality, superiority, and autonomy with respect to Him, just after they had been created. Thus, separation from God is just a step away. The two take that step and they find themselves separated from each other and from God.

Can you say more about this separation from God?

By *separation*, we mean above all *inequality*: God is the sea; the human being is a pail. In their state of complete spiritual infancy, Adam and Eve were deceived into grasping prematurely at something they were meant to receive gradually — over the course of centuries and centuries — as God revealed Himself to humanity in a way that *measured* their happiness to their capacity and prepared them for the incursion of divine love. And yet, they were tempted to be *like God*!

By persuading them to consume, all at once, knowledge of good and evil — and knowledge of God — under conditions for which they were entirely unprepared, the devil *abused* them. He enticed them to taste, far too soon, the sweetness of divine wisdom, the fullness of which they and their descendants would never cease to seek thereafter — chasing after images, models, and surrogates rather than the divine Original. But God is not some common apple, easily bitten and chewed in a few quick bites to be *fully* tasted and assimilated.

The tempter dangled before them mere lanterns, and they, in their innocence, delighted in them — though they themselves were already fireflies, shining with the light they had been given. While the Lord God had established, in wisdom and love, a covenant with man and woman, the *killjoy* shattered the joyful harmony between them and their Creator, distorting the very *icon* of God, man, and woman in communion. By falsifying God's identity — and, in turn, the identity of man and woman — he succeeded in introducing division, anguish, toil, suffering, and death into human existence.

Later, Scripture gives the tempter the name *Satan* (from the Hebrew term meaning "adversary"), which corresponds to *devil* (from the Greek *diabolos*: "the one who sows discord, accusation, calumny, deceit, and leads to error"). The devil — Satan — is not merely an image, a symbol, or a myth, but a *real* being, actively at work in leading humanity toward evil.

Throughout salvation history, Israel — and, through Israel, all of humanity — takes on the figure of a woman, at times of extraordinary beauty in her fidelity to God, and at other times lost in idolatry. In turning away from God, both Israel and humanity have sought *idols*, which Scripture identifies as demons — active rivals of

God. In their most extreme rejection of the divine, they even offered human sacrifices to these idols, on the high places where they were worshipped. Yet Our Lord continually seeks them out — not by violating the freedom of the creatures He willed and loves, but by calling them back, again and again, to restore the original covenant with Israel and, through Israel, with all of humanity.

Why does the devil always suggest wanting "to be like God"?

Man and woman ought to have acted as the man Jesus did, recognizing before the Father, "a body hast thou prepared for me" (Heb. 10:5) — in other words, acknowledging their *limit* and accepting their humanity as finite in relation to the divine nature.

To surpass the Pillars of Hercules, which mark the boundaries of human limitation, is to presume to become the sole arbiter of good and evil, severed from any ethical or transcendent reference. This reflects an insatiable desire to *go beyond*, a refusal to be content with one's human condition.

Such an impulse is both deceptive and destructive, for it never truly attains its goal and quickly spirals out of control. In the end, it distorts the very meaning of good and evil, of the human and the divine. Writing to the Christians in Rome, St. Paul describes those who have fallen into such arrogance: "They exchanged the glory of the immortal God for images resembling mortal man or birds or animals or reptiles" (Rom. 1:23).

As G. Ragozzino writes, "From the attempt to penetrate the impenetrable are born what we call 'the occult sciences'" — a kind of *hidden knowledge* believed to be attainable through means outside the realm of legitimate science.

Many, in their pride, exalt freedom, autonomy, and progress while exploiting the credulity of the simple to subject them to evil, as well as to the devil and his cunning deceptions. In doing so, they imitate the fallen angel, seeking to elevate themselves as a power that would dominate both individuals and the universe itself.

Fr. Amorth obtained his degree in law and was ordained a priest in the Society of St. Paul. He is a renowned conference lecturer and spiritual guide.

CHAPTER SIX

One Who Does Not Sleep at Night

"The devil prowls like a roaring lion, looking for someone to devour."[18]

In which other Scripture passages is he called a "killjoy"?

During His public ministry, the Divine Master warned of *a man* who goes about under cover of night, sowing weeds in the grain fields of others. Jesus' power over evil was unmistakable — His casting out of demons from the oppressed demonstrated, in concrete reality, His authority to expel unclean spirits, forgive sins, and heal the sick.

He freed many possessed individuals from the grip of the devil's oppression. "Behold, I cast out demons," He assures, before sending His disciples to do the same. In certain episodes, the Master's healing of the afflicted — restoring them to wholeness by liberating them from the evil one — takes the form of true exorcisms, revealing His dominion over both the physical and spiritual realms.

Who demonstrated that the devil can be defeated?

Jesus Christ, obviously. The Son of God made man manifests Himself as the one who vanquishes and repulses the evil one.

Although He knew no sin, He knows its external seductions and the sufferings of temptation. When the Holy Spirit made an

---

[18] 1 Peter 5:8.

appointment with the tempter, Jesus personally confronted Satan before beginning His public ministry. He was tempted in the desert, considered the dwelling place of evil spirits, as well as the place of solitude and temptation.

How did Jesus confront Satan?

Luke's Gospel reports the episode of Jesus' temptations, which Mark only mentions in passing, and Matthew proposes it in richer detail. "Temptation was a real experience for Jesus," we read in number 182 and following of the *Adult Catechism*: "He 'was tested in everything, similar to us, except in sin' (Heb. 4:15). … Jesus entrusts Himself to the mysterious fidelity of the Father and adheres constantly to His will (cf. Heb. 5:8), without the least hesitation; He defeats Satan in the strength of the Holy Spirit; and He reestablishes the primordial harmony with all of creation, from the angels to the animals, like Adam in the Garden of Eden."

Both the temptation carried out by the devil as well as Jesus' response are narrated through use of the Word of God. This makes it clear that temptation as well as the Word are to be taken very seriously. Jesus' recourse to Sacred Scripture constitutes the decisive argument to shut the devil's mouth: "It is written" is repeated three times by the Lord as a response to the temptations.

We know, however, that the Son of God *is the Word made flesh* and has excellent knowledge of the written Word. Having assured protection and life ("He [God] will give His angels charge of you, to guard you in all your ways. On their hands they will bear you up, lest you dash your foot against a stone" [Ps. 91:11–12]), Jesus Christ is the Word of fidelity to the Father, given that He definitively rejects evil and the tempter unto death on the Cross: "For the joy that was set before Him He endured the Cross, despising the shame" (Heb. 12:2). When tempted to deviate from the Father's plan in favor of an earthly and political messianism and for an ephemeral good, the Lord responds by professing the one true God. He is not as the devil would like to diminish Him, nor as the world would expect Him to be, but He starkly opposes its mentality and expectations.

Why was Jesus tempted first to obtain food?

Jesus was tempted by the same things that ordinarily tempt human beings. First, He was tempted to seek nourishment outside of God's plan and His divine word — just as the people of God were tempted in the desert, as recounted in the book of Deuteronomy. The first temptation concerns one's personal, physical, bodily needs: Jesus was hungry. This is *the temptation of bread.*

Providing for one's basic needs is not, in itself, evil, nor is it inherently a diabolical temptation. The temptation lies in demanding that God provide miraculously rather than through the natural order of human effort. It is the desire to secure food, health, and material goods by bypassing labor — exploiting circumstances, privileges, or even putting God to the test instead of using one's own abilities and virtues. Jesus, however, did not come into the world to guarantee material provision through miracles. Rather, He came to proclaim "the kingdom of God and his righteousness" (Matt. 6:33), as the Gospel affirms.

How does the second temptation come about?

The second temptation takes place within society, in the social context. Jesus is led into the city, where He is urged to perform a miracle to gain recognition — throwing Himself down from the temple parapet so that God might save Him.

Satan's proposals align with the expectations of Jesus' social environment; they reflect what people in every age instinctively desire for their own fulfillment — recognition, status, and admiration.

Undoubtedly, what weighs most heavily on human beings is often not suffering itself, but the dull monotony of daily life — the dust of routine, the anonymity of one's surroundings, the boredom of repetitive tasks, the endless hours passing without miracles. Deprived of certain kinds of recognition, applause, or public validation, some begin to feel as though they are nothing.

This leads to the temptation to *be noticed at any cost* — to make oneself the center of attention, even when doing so requires spectacle or artificial self-promotion. It is the lure of treating life as a stage, of performing for the world's gaze, often in ways unworthy even of the theater, grasping at fleeting glory. How many compromises do people make simply to be seen, when they fail to recognize the value of their own history and dignity?

For the sake of power and vainglory, some are willing to *sell their soul to Satan*, without turning even briefly to God.

But the Son of God already *knows* the One who recognizes Him; He has no need to seek attention for its own sake.

This temptation struck Jesus with particular violence during His Passion, when He was seized by the anguish of human weakness before death. In that moment, He faced the temptation to come down from the Cross and *prove* His divine power — to perform the ultimate spectacle. Yet He remained, embracing His mission fully, resisting the fleeting triumph of self-display for the eternal victory of obedience to the Father.

Can you say more about Jesus' miracles?

Jesus of Nazareth displayed His unmistakable style even in the way He performed miracles. As the Son, steadfast in rejecting temptations to wealth, success, and power, He never used miracles for His own personal benefit — never to relieve His own hunger, thirst, or exhaustion, nor to display His divinity for spectacle. He conducted Himself as a mere man and a believer, relying not on divine power to defeat the tempter but solely on His trust in the Father.

He consistently refused demands for extraordinary signs meant to compel belief. He even forbade those He healed from publicizing their miracles.

"Miracles, of course, are not sufficient to produce faith: it is the interior attraction to the Father that arouses it," we read in the *Adult Catechism*, no. 194. Nor are miracles the primary salvific events: The true bread is not what He multiplied, but the eucharistic bread; the true light is not what was restored to the man born blind, but the light of our baptismal Faith.

How can one explain the third temptation?

The third temptation takes place on the mountain, a symbol of the place where God's greatest revelations occur — Sinai, Nebo, Horeb, Tabor, Calvary — where humanity is called to make the radical choice between good and evil, between God and the devil. Here, in the presence of the tempter, Jesus pronounces His *yes* — not to Satan, but to the Father, as His beloved and blessed Son. Having overcome the devil, the angels draw near to serve Him, while the defeated adversary departs, humiliated.

This temptation on the mountain mirrors the trials we face in the temple, in the sanctuary, in the Church itself — where our relationship with God is directly assailed, where our outward religiosity can be tested against the authenticity of our Faith and our acceptance of the divine *free gift*. It is this divine gift that allows us to experience God the Father in joy, producing results entirely new and unique compared to the rigid demands of the ancient divine command and the eventual rejection of it by the first man and woman when they faced the tempter.

Is Jesus' behavior in overcoming the temptations and fending off the devil paradigmatic for us?

We too can succumb to the tempter's influence — to the forcefulness of temptation and to the overwhelming sense of God's absence when we are put to the test. Worse still, in the midst of temptation, we may feel as though God's favor has been withdrawn, that we are left to face the trial alone. When this happens, we endure temptation in confusion, at our weakest, most vulnerable, and most likely to fall.

It is precisely in such spiritual crises that the seductive catechism of the tempter finds its foothold: "Don't deceive yourself, God is not there, He does not love you."

In His encounter with the tempter, Jesus first seeks to convince those who doubt that the possibility of being tempted is real. By revealing Himself as the victor over temptation, He also demonstrates the conditions of His victory: total abandonment to the Father. Whether in the three temptations in the solitude of the desert or in the final, terrible trial on the Cross, the Savior experiences above all the *apparent* distance of God — to the point of crying out, "My God, my God, why hast thou forsaken me?" (Ps. 22:1).

Yet even in this, He entrusts Himself to the Father with absolute confidence: "Father, into thy hands I commit my spirit!" (Luke 23:46), certain that He is not truly abandoned, even in the moment of death.

This is the great testimony of Jesus for us: In temptation and in our greatest trials — when the tempter makes his final assault at the hour of death — we need only surrender ourselves into the arms of God the Father.

In this way, Christ's victory over the devil becomes more than just a triumph — it becomes an example for us, a paradigm for how to face every kind of temptation.

What should be our interior disposition for enduring trials?

To entrust ourselves freely to the love of the Father — to experience that love and adopt the filial attitude of Jesus — we need the fullness of faith, much time, intense prayer, and a profound, personal Paschal experience of death and resurrection. This transformation shifts us from the status of a servant to the fulfilling identity of a son.

Trials bring about this transformation. It is not so much the Lord who convinces us, but rather we who come to recognize for ourselves that He is near and loves us as a Father. Ordinarily, these are interior trials — not divine punishments, but the natural means by which the heavenly Father leads His children to maturity.

The son who is pleasing to God the Father is one who can face evil and the cross with fortitude, precisely because he knows that the Father is present in his trials, sustaining him. Thus, the Father's joy is in seeing His son reach full maturity, able to face even the cross and death when they come. The son, in turn, finds joy in realizing that the Father shares in his suffering, that He is present and will not abandon him.

To stand against evil and the evil one, we must undergo training, strengthening the "muscles" of our interior life through practice. We must endure this reality day and night and confront evil directly. If we erase from our minds the terror, the darkness, and the all-too-real presence of one who extracts poisons from the flowers of evil, we will become spineless — weak in life, cowardly in the face of adversity and death. In truth, we will already be dead before we die.

What purpose does the devil serve in God's plan?

Once upon a time, the devil was depicted in the most repulsive manner, adorned with fearsome masks meant to deter. In the past, such imagery was common. Today, however, these depictions seem almost *ridiculous* — claws and horns appearing here and there. At most, such "deterrence" might startle the weak from their slumber, but in a civilization so steeped in horror that we have all grown accustomed to it, such images are easily dismissed. In the end, by fixating on the image of the *beast*, we become desensitized to it and lose sight of its reality.

Exposure to evil — through newspapers, television, and advertising — gradually numbs public perception of the devil, diluting his presence, leading many to ignore him, or even deceiving themselves into believing he does not exist. This is precisely the goal of those who want us to forget the one who threatens us, who throws a wrench into the workings of God and goodness.

His followers continue to *hide* him beneath alluring appearances and lavish disguises. The manipulators of this world, particularly certain media lobbies, seek to obscure the reality of evil through so-called *reality shows* (which are, in truth, anything but real), subtly embodying the devil while falsifying his identity — ultimately erasing him from our consciousness. Only strong spirits resist this phenomenon, reawakening within themselves true humanity, interiority, rational thought, knowledge, and an awareness of reality. These are the souls who can stand against evil, trusting in goodness, in humanity, and in God.

Certain "heroes" of our time bear no resemblance to the intrepid explorers who once charted unknown seas and tamed savage continents. They have nothing in common with those great figures who stood ready to fight real enemies, not mere phantoms. Nor can they be compared to the martyrs who faced wild beasts and, before that, resisted the temptations of demons — mocking them in triumph. These past generations, even without the comforts we take for granted, braved untamed lands, endured life's tempests, and confronted pain and misfortune with courage. They understood that existence is not merely warmth and comfort, but that evil is real — and at times, even the ancient serpent must be faced.

In a certain sense, we might say that the devil's *greatest* work is offering us the very *opportunity* for battle. His presence and activity in the world keep us vigilant, training us for the fight. We must take his existence seriously, drawing on objective and credible sources that testify to his presence and works. We must *memorize him interiorly*, foreseeing his moves — without deluding ourselves into thinking we can simply exhaust him or make him disappear. Whether he has horns, a tail, a beak, or the features of a fallen angel (as Alessandro Baricco suggests), or worse, whether he is recognized as an intellect of pure and terrible brilliance, we must not be deceived.

CHAPTER SEVEN

"It Is by the Finger of God That I Cast out Demons"[19]

"Behold, I cast out demons and perform cures today and tomorrow, and the third day I finish my course."[20]

Seeing the insolence and upper-handedness of evil, can we not suspect that God shows Himself in weakness?

If we are being honest, the overwhelming darkness of daily news reports might make it seem as though evil reigns unchecked. Newspapers and television relentlessly highlight the most disturbing crimes, simply because such stories reflect a significant portion of daily reality. As I have said before: If it rains, I cannot pretend the sky is blue.

What stands out, however, is the partiality of many journalists, who ignore the other side of reality — the events that could just as well be called *good news* if they were reported. They justify this omission, as we have seen, by claiming that stories of things going well do not capture public attention.

Amid the constant stream of crime and tragedy, it seems as though the presence, goodness, and power of God are in the minority. If we analyze the facts as they are presented, it might even appear that God Himself is discouraged and cast aside. The impression given is that He once tried to set things right but has since

---

[19] Luke 11:20.
[20] Luke 13:32.

abandoned the effort — weak, absent, withdrawn from the world, perhaps never having been present at all.

So what can be done: Should we stop turning to God?

People today undoubtedly feel the weight of evil, especially since it is emphasized far more than the light yoke of goodness. The triumph of evil dominates the news, making its vocabulary more familiar to us. People are ruled by it — they live it, suffer under it, and are provoked by it. At times, it seems we are so overwhelmed by evil that we resign ourselves to its inevitability. As Martin Luther King once said, "We have learned to fly like the birds and swim like fish, but we still have not learned to live like brothers."

And yet, in the face of this, how can we not think of God? What do we lose by allowing ourselves to be drawn to Him and led by Him?

To make us partakers in His eternal love, the Most Holy Trinity, from all eternity, willed that we should taste that love through His Son, sent into the world. Overflowing with divine love, the Father *imagines*, *plans*, and *creates* from all eternity a universe worthy of receiving His Son.

Consider, if you will forgive the comparison, Leonardo da Vinci painting the *Mona Lisa* (*La Gioconda*). Before him was the face, the eyes, the very soul of the modest and gentle woman he was capturing with genius on his canvas. Likewise, as I have said, in the workshop of the Trinity, not only is the aesthetic subject realized, but also the *Original* of all the subsequent and infinite divine works. The Father is creating, shaping, sculpting, and painting all things, visible and invisible. In doing so, He contemplates the Son, who will become the most beautiful of the sons of men, passing among us first as a son, then as the suffering one, crucified, risen, and glorified.

The creation of God's first and most wondrous work, as well as the ongoing, providential unfolding of creation, takes place in the contemplation of the Son, "the only-begotten God, who is in the bosom of the Father," as we read in the Prologue of John's Gospel.

Creation in Christ did not happen in some distant past but is made real each day in the gift of divine Providence, who entrusts goodness to every human being. It is up to us to *perceive* this goodness in its *original form*, which is Jesus Christ — crucified and risen, teacher and shepherd, victorious over evil and the spirits of darkness. And in the rest of humanity, too, we see this same pattern: crucified and risen.

Why did the devil have to end up on earth?

In the book of Revelation, St. John the Evangelist writes:

> War arose in heaven, Michael and his angels fighting against the dragon; and the dragon and his angels fought, but they were defeated and there was no longer any place for them in heaven. And the great dragon was thrown down, that ancient serpent, who is called the devil and Satan, the deceiver of the whole world — he was thrown down to the earth, and his angels were thrown down with him. (Rev. 12:7–9)

This battle, of course, was fought with spiritual weapons. God created all celestial spirits free, and thus He could not compel them to love Him. But while the rebellious angels gradually lost their attraction to God, the faithful angels grew ever more drawn to Him, their devotion intensifying. Those who chose to remain on His side came to partake of His divine essence, and for this reason, the angels led by the Archangel Michael can never rebel against the Lord — their enjoyment of

His essence makes any turning away impossible. Likewise, in paradise, we too will live wholly in God.

The heavenly spirits who refused to remain with God grew cold in intellect, will, and love, becoming so spiritually deformed that they ultimately severed themselves from Him and fell to the earth. According to biblical tradition, once on earth, demons came to inhabit tombs of the dead, deserts, ruins, and cursed places — such as Babylon and the lands of Edom, once known for their enmity toward God's people. There, they became mingled with dark presences, wild beasts, and swine.

How does the devil act in the world?

Jesus Himself calls the devil "the prince of this world" (John 14:30). St. Paul describes him as "the god of this world" (2 Cor. 4:4), emphasizing that, as a deceiver by nature, he is capable of disguising himself, assuming divine traits in order to obscure the truth. To mislead people into error and sin, Satan — "whose intentions are well known" (2 Cor. 2:11) — "disguises himself as an angel of light" (2 Cor. 11:14), as the Apostle warns. Likewise, St. John states, "the whole world is in the power of the evil one" (1 John 5:19), meaning by world everything that stands in opposition to God.

Because of His particular experience of Christ, St. Paul expands the temporal scope of this mystery of iniquity, making clear that it is already at work — not embodied in any single individual, but rooted in its true and ultimate source: "the prince of the power of the air, the spirit that is now at work in the sons of disobedience" (Eph. 2:2). He further clarifies the devil's identity, warning that "we are not contending against flesh and blood, but against the principalities, against the powers, against the world rulers of this present darkness, against the spiritual hosts of wickedness in the heavenly places" (Eph. 6:12).

Paul makes it clear, then, that rebellious human beings — especially the powerful of this world — are subjected to a higher authority: the spirits of the air, to whom their worship and sacrifices are ultimately directed. Not only those who actively participate in such rites fall under these powers, but also those who passively allow such worship to take place.

Thus, Paul strongly asserts the irreconcilable opposition between worship directed to Christ and that offered to demons. Whoever does not venerate Christ inevitably venerates idols and spirits, just as the mystery religions of every age have done — especially those that flourished in the Greco-Roman world. "What pagans sacrifice they offer to demons and not to God," Paul declares. "I do not want you to be partners with demons. You cannot drink the cup of the Lord and the cup of demons. You cannot partake of the table of the Lord and the table of demons" (1 Cor. 10:20–21). And again:

> What partnership have righteousness and iniquity? Or what fellowship has light with darkness? What accord has Christ with Belial? Or what has a believer in common with an unbeliever? What agreement has the temple of God with idols? For we are the temple of the living God. (2 Cor. 6:14–16)

Thus, these putrefied angels, these angels gone bad, wage war against those who believe in Christ. After the battle between Michael's followers and those of Lucifer, as we read in Revelation: "the dragon … went off to make war on the rest of her offspring, on those who keep the commandments of God and bear testimony to Jesus" (Rev. 12:17). Knowing that "his time is short" (Rev. 12:12) and that he will ultimately be "thrown into the lake of fire and brimstone" (Rev. 20:10), the devil does everything in his power to draw as many souls to himself as possible. And at times, he succeeds.

Does God give a free hand to the devil, then?

St. Augustine holds that if the devil were given free rein by God, "none of us would remain alive."

"The power of Satan is, nonetheless, not infinite," we read in paragraph 395 of the *Catechism of the Catholic Church*. "He is only a creature, powerful from the fact that he is pure spirit, but still a creature. He cannot prevent the building up of God's reign. Although Satan may act in the world out of hatred for God and His kingdom in Christ Jesus, and although his action may cause grave injuries — of a spiritual nature and, indirectly, even of a physical nature — to each man and to society, the action is permitted by divine providence, which with strength and gentleness guides human and cosmic history. It is a great mystery that providence should permit diabolical activity, but 'we know that in everything God works for the good of those who love Him' " (Rom. 8:28).

Thus, we entrust ourselves to Jesus Christ, the Son of God made man, who came "to destroy the works of the devil" (1 John 3:8) and to free us human beings, who were enslaved to Satan. Jesus Christ casts out demons "by the finger of God" (Luke 11:20), meaning that He has the power to bind Satan, stripping him of everything — even his kingdom, which is coming to an end. He continues this work today through the Church and through priestly exorcists: "Behold, I cast out demons and perform cures today and tomorrow, and the third day I finish my course" (Luke 13:32).

We can therefore rest assured that we have on our side both the Strong One and the Church, as we shall see in a moment.

Why did God grant so much power to the devil?

Allow me to preface my response. Just as God the Father and the Holy Spirit united the Son to human nature — so that the Son of Man might *experience* the weakness of the flesh, love it, and redeem it as the *Strong One* even unto death on the Cross — so too did He ordain that human beings should be accompanied by the angel of darkness, that they might come to esteem the power given them in bearing and confronting the forces of evil as mature sons.

Ultimately, this power was granted in Christ, who draws and strengthens both heavenly spirits and human beings. The latter, through their intelligence and freedom — neither of which is ordered toward evil — attain spiritual adulthood precisely by confronting and overcoming the devil.

For this reason, if the entire unity of creation is oriented toward Christ, then evil and the devil cannot be permitted to prevail over good, and even less so over God Himself, given Christ's centrality. Moreover, Satan's rebellion — his desire to be first in all things — and his consequent defeat serve as a restraint, preventing human beings from falling into the same temptation of rivalry with God.

At the conclusion of a series of exorcisms, it is fitting to recite the Christological hymn from the Letter to the Philippians (2:6–11). At the proclamation that "at the name of Jesus every knee should bow, in heaven and on earth and under the earth" (Phil. 2:10), both the exorcist and those present kneel, and the possessed person is always compelled to do the same. There is no escape: The demon must bow before Christ, who is victorious over evil and all who serve it.

Sacred Scripture makes clear that at times it is God Himself who afflicts human beings with various hardships — plagues, fevers, and even the sending of the angel of destruction, an evil spirit, or Satan. In the book of Job, we read that at first the Creator placed all that Job possessed into the devil's power, forbidding the tempter, however, from laying a hand on his person; later, He permitted Satan to afflict even Job's body, but only on the condition that his life be spared.

The devil's ordinary mode of action is to tempt human beings to do evil. As has been reiterated, even Jesus submitted to the devil's temptations and overcame them. For had He succumbed, it would have been like renouncing a treasure for a counterfeit coin. What could the devil offer Jesus that the Lord did not already possess? Though Satan knew that the Only Begotten Son in the bosom of the Father could not sin — since He is Goodness itself — he harassed Him nonetheless, aiming (though in vain) to *deform* Christ's image before the world. Yet Christ is the one of whom Scripture says, "You are the most handsome of the sons of men" (Ps. 45:2).

For this reason, God tempts no one to evil, for He has a natural abhorrence of it. Rather, He incites us to goodness and at times permits trials that we might be spiritually purified, freed from our imperfections, and made steadfast in our desire for the good. He allows us to be filled with divine love in proportion to our capacity to receive it — whether like a glass or a barrel, small or great — so that in life and in goodness, nothing may be lacking to us.

Thus, the Lord allows the devil to tempt us, but never beyond our strength. The devil may seek to lead a man into evil, but only because God permits it and only for a short time — so that the man, having gained experience, may overcome evil together with Christ and surrender himself fully to God the Father.

In this way, God does not impose His love, though He ardently desires to love us. He does not force His gift upon us — neither in the beginning nor throughout the course of human history. He first offers Himself in Christ, then at the end of time, and finally, face to face, just as He is.

Does evil harm God or human beings more?

Sin takes nothing away from God. Nor, I would say, does it offend Him or cast Him in a poor light, for God's recognition and glory do not depend on the thoughts or actions of His creatures. In reality, evil harms the one who commits it even before it afflicts its victim. St. Paul describes this as death — a death that consists in the loss of God, who desires to give Himself to humanity in love. Once a person has truly tasted God's goodness in an intense way, even after being forgiven for his transgressions, he can only long to be filled with the divine presence, truth, and love.

The final blow suffered by evil has the power to disillusion those who had deceived themselves into believing they could *keep God in their pocket* — along with Eden, absolute discernment of good and evil, and the supposed right and autonomy to impose them. Once a person recognizes his human limits before God, and before good and evil, he finds true and lasting peace in God.

If someone in the past has been more reckless than Dennis the Menace and, even after his conversion, still believes he has not been fully forgiven, justified, or saved — if he carries within his soul an exhausting sense of guilt — he must know that all this suffering, born of rebellion, transgression, and sin, has truly come to an end in the arms of the Son of God, God the Father, and God the Holy Spirit. The Trinity, united and present within each of us, dwelling in our hearts, has already loved, redeemed, and blessed him.

Likewise, if a devout spirit, eager to lead the converted into ever greater piety, believes in the rigid idea of God that he has constructed for himself — measuring others by his own *height* and keeping a meticulous account of his religious observance — let him understand this: to be loved by God, he no longer needs to *pay* Him or establish fixed times and places to meet Him. For it is God who has already chosen to draw near and *inhabit* him from the very beginning.

Where does the devil get to work?

Evil is present *in reality* and therefore also *in the human being*. I try my hardest to be "human," "good," and a bit "saintly," but I don't always succeed. If I don't succeed, it means that *something is not right in me*. Thus, I might struggle to welcome the *heaven* that is in me and love myself; and so I tend more easily to notice *hell* and the devil.

What I mean is that by knowing ourselves, we can truly perceive within not only the bad part, the hell within us, but also the beautiful aspect, heaven. To extinguish evil, we think we have only a pail of water, when actually a whole squadron of firefighters is at our service. Our positive potential is great.

Thus, we can live more peacefully, more happily, because we know how things stand, at least within us: beloved and blessed by our Lord as well as being equipped with good things.

Who saves us from the power of Satan?

The universe finds its origin and meaning in light of the "Word with God" and of the "Only Son of God, who is in the bosom of the Father" (John 1:1, 18).

As we have said, God loves, creates, and protects the universe and humanity by *contemplating* the Son as their form and model. It is within this *Christocentric* vision of God's plan that the creature assumes his proper place, recognized as *very good* (Gen. 1:31), and therefore as something precious, worthy of being defended and saved from evil and the tempter. This is why the Father can only love us and protect us from evil, to the point of allowing Jesus Christ to die and rise again for us and for all.

It is the death and Resurrection of Christ that give strength to humanity in general, and to Christians in particular, in their struggle against evil. Every time we look upon the crucifix, the first word that should come to our lips is *Thank You!* And so, we surrender ourselves to the Father, the Son, and the Holy Spirit.

Is He the Savior, then?

In coming into the world, the Son did not lose His divinity. He demonstrates this through His miracles, His Transfiguration, and His Resurrection after death. To make clear that Jesus remains the Son of God even in His humanity — and thus to show that evil, the devil, and the world have no power over Him — the evangelists employ an interesting narrative pattern: Whenever it seems that the Lord's divinity is obscured, diminished, or in need of reaffirmation, angels or extraordinary signs always appear. This occurs at His Incarnation, His birth, His Baptism in the Jordan, His trials in the desert, His agony in Gethsemane, and at the tomb after His Resurrection.

The Son of God came into the world — a world that is *very good*, insofar as it is the work of God, the dwelling place of God, and beloved by God. Jesus was its redeeming Messiah. He became man not to judge or condemn the world or the present age, but because evil entered the world through the work of the devil and man. As a result, the world is also a society of sinners — those who reject salvation, persecute Jesus, and condemn both Him and His disciples.

Jesus Christ the Lord came to save the world because it is subject to Satan and, for this reason, does not recognize God and stands in need of salvation, awaiting its final redemption. The Lord accomplished our salvation because evil, the devil, and the world have no power over Him. He reigns over the world; He has conquered it, for its wisdom is foolishness before God. It is folly and enmity that ultimately dissipates — just as the world itself is passing away. And so, while Jesus and His disciples are *in* the world, they are not *of* the world.

There is, then, a salvific purpose in the mission of Christ Jesus: He enters the world, suffers, and dies, removing every separation between God and humanity, revealing the love of the Father. The Son does not simply perform a rite — He gives Himself.

In this *giving*, the debt and the offering that religion once required as a duty to God were brought to an end. In Christ Jesus, the Jewish, Christian, religious fast is fulfilled: fasting for God, offering to Him, dying for Him. No longer is it man who must die for God; rather, it is God who has given Himself for man. For this reason, there is no further need for a mediator, priesthood, sacrifice, or expiation to take Christ's place. God asks for no further "sacrifice or oblation" (Dan. 3:38). The offering is complete, fulfilled in Christ Jesus, in whom we have access to the Father as His children: "My son, you are always with Me, and everything that is Mine is yours" (Luke 15:31).

It is in this intimate covenant between the Father and the Son that our *peace with God* is definitively revealed and realized. All that remains for us is to remember it, celebrate it, live it, and allow it to overflow within us — sharing it with all.

What power do the Virgin Mary and the apostles have against Satan?

In the divine plan of salvation, the Creator's thought and love for the Virgin Mary could not be absent — for she is the one in whom the incarnation of the Son of God was to be realized.

The Immaculate Virgin, whose offspring would crush the head of the tempter, was united with the Son in the battle to definitively defeat the devil. This is assured in chapter 12 of the book of Revelation.

The Mother is entirely united to the divine Son in the work of salvation. As Vatican II reaffirms, "Mary devoted herself totally as a handmaid of the Lord to the person and work of her Son, under Him and with Him, by the grace of almighty God, serving the mystery of redemption" (*Lumen Gentium* 56). Even today, the Son and the Mother remain united in the struggle against evil in the world, particularly in sustaining the work of exorcists.

As is well known, Christ Jesus has power over demons and continues to subjugate the kingdom of Satan. For this reason, the Gospels emphasize Jesus' exorcisms — His liberation of those possessed by demons, those who were "under the power of the devil" (Acts 10:38).

It is clear, then, why the first power Jesus gives to the apostles is that of casting out demons. Although they were called by the Master "to be with Him" (Mark 3:14) and sent out into the world, they are in the world but not of the world — a world that does not know them and hates them. They are like lambs, suffering persecution, while the sons of this world rejoice, cunning as ravenous wolves. Yet those whom Jesus sends, who are from God, conquer the world, for they are prudent as serpents and simple as doves, awaiting the final judgment and God's verdict against the world of evil — when the goats (the wicked) and the sheep (the righteous) will be separated, and the saints will judge the world.

Jesus assures us that the task of resisting and casting out the devil belongs not only to priests but also to ordinary Christians: "And these signs will accompany those who believe: in My name they will cast out demons" (Mark 16:17). The later institution of the ministry of exorcist — reserved to priests — did not negate Christ's gift of this power to the faithful. Rather, the faithful continue to have at their disposal effective, indispensable, and commonly accessible means of grace: prayer, the sacraments, penance, works of charity, and private prayers of deliverance.

It remains the duty of all to denounce, combat, and drive out evil and the causes that unleash it — both within ourselves and in the world. We cannot absolve ourselves of this responsibility. Christians know that they do not fight alone; many have already suffered and struggled for the sake of righteousness. And One did so unto death — the Son of God, our Brother and Master.

Filled with goodness, nourished by the overwhelming experience of the unmerited love of God the Father, the Son, and the Holy Spirit, we too — like Jesus — can overcome diabolical temptation with resolve. Yet this victory is not merely the fruit of ethical determination; it is the result of the superabundant gift we have received, which instills in us both a repugnance for evil and a decisive rejection of the one who embodies it.

To what extent do our own powers and observance of God's law save us?

Salvation, promised once to Abraham before the gift of the Law, is granted to all in Jesus Christ, who is not merely a faithful servant but the beloved Son of the Father. Jesus recognized that the old wineskins of the Law of Sinai could not contain the new wine of the Gospel, because its commands had become an end in themselves, hardening hearts rather than fostering the joy of commitment and the power of the Spirit. This power is fully present in the person and teaching of the new Master and Guide, who surpasses Moses. For this reason, He is the only Teacher whose *yoke* is light; He can be followed, and His word put into practice, because He reveals the Father's tenderness.

All of this is directed toward making us "participants in the divine nature" (2 Pet. 1:4), "sons of the Most High" (Ps. 82:6), and "sons of God" (Gal. 3:26). St. Paul affirms this clearly: "For in Christ Jesus you are all sons of God, through faith. For as many of you as were baptized into Christ have put on Christ" (Gal. 3:26–27). At its core, a golden thread runs through all of Sacred Scripture: "I have loved you with an everlasting love" (Jer. 31:3). So much so that, writing to the Christians in Galatia, Paul testifies: "Jesus Christ gave Himself for me" (Gal. 2:20).

Regarding the observance of the Law, St. Paul combats an idea and a practice that treated human obedience to the divine Law as a guarantee of the love and salvation that come from God.

Based on his own experience, the Apostle recognizes that the Law, as it was being interpreted in his time, posed the danger of making human righteousness before God depend not on God's free gift, but on the fulfillment of commandments and good works. In such a system, the just man, by virtue of his obedience to the Law, would supposedly have the right to be loved and saved by God.

Yet, according to Sacred Scripture, even the righteous man sins seven times a day. St. Paul therefore insists that no one can observe the Law perfectly and at all times; all sin and are incapable of saving themselves. He thus concludes that it is *God's gift* that saves us. The gratuitous love of God overflows in Christ and is first poured into those who receive Him. The Christian, knowing himself to be loved by the Lord without any price, responds by doing good and observing all the norms of goodness that God and life itself present to him.

The novelty of Christianity, then, does not lie in the abolition of the Law and the commandments of God, but in their *fulfillment*. This fulfillment consists in the Christian's deeper, even *visceral*, motivations that enable him to live according to them. Because he has experienced the divine gift, he knows that God the Father has loved him *first* and freely. Drawn by this love, he can respond by keeping God's commandments, which are expressions of love, praying in the words of the Psalmist: "I give thanks to Thy name for Thy steadfast love and Thy faithfulness" (Ps. 138:2).

With his meek temperament, Fr. Gabriele draws strength from the Divine Master in combat against the devil, above all through prayer.

CHAPTER EIGHT

"Do Not Resist the Evil One"

*"Do not return evil for evil or reviling for reviling;
but on the contrary bless, for this you have been
called, that you may obtain a blessing."*[21]

Who is the evil one, according to Sacred Scripture?

The wicked are often identified most clearly by those who consider themselves *pure*. The book of Wisdom states, "Their wickedness blinded them, and they did not know the secret purposes of God" (Wis. 2:21–22). Similarly, in the book of Jeremiah, the man of the Bible turns to God with a question: "Why does the way of the wicked prosper? Why do all who are treacherous thrive?" (Jer. 12:1). At one point, he even suspects that God Himself might be complicit in the schemes of the wicked: "Thou plantest them, and they take root." Yet he soon corrects himself, acknowledging, "Thou art near in their mouth and far from their heart" (Jer. 12:2).

Jesus Himself clashed with the wicked — those who saw Him as an evildoer, despised Him, slandered Him, and ultimately rejected Him to the point of putting Him to death. Arrested as a brigand, He was spat upon, struck by soldiers, and mocked: "Prophesy to us, you Christ! Who is it that struck you?" (Matt. 26:68). He was crowned with thorns, nailed to the Cross, and then taunted once more: "If you are the Son of God, come down from the Cross" (Matt. 27:40).

---

[21]   1 Peter 3:9.

Why have so many turned evil throughout the ages?

Even in our time, the *killjoys* dominate the narrative, filling newspapers and television series with crime stories. There are certainly many ways in which the evil one wreaks havoc. But the real question we must ask is not how, but why — why do such evildoers exist at all, and what has corrupted them to this degree?

When we seek explanations, we quickly find ourselves in deep waters, tangled in a web of worldly causes — psychological, social, environmental, or even religious. Some will go so far as to argue that, in rare cases, wickedness is genetic.

While we may still think, as the Pharisees in the Gospel of John did, "This crowd does not know the law; they are accursed" (John 7:49), Jesus offers a much deeper explanation: The wicked "know not what they do" (Luke 23:34) and act as they do "because they do not know Him who sent Me" (John 15:21), that is, the Father. This reason supersedes all others. Indeed, not knowing the Father is the greatest of all evils.

Applied to the *demonic* behavior of many individuals today, the absence — and therefore, the lack of knowledge — of the father (in the biological sense) opens a deep and painful void in sons, leaving them vulnerable to deviation, delinquency, and outright wickedness.

Today, this state of unrest and suffering is no longer merely individual — it has become collective. In such a world, many seek refuge in sexual license, fleeting relationships, cohabitation, divorce, and serial marriages. Lacking an awareness of the sacredness of being sons — and thus fathers and mothers — they live disconnected lives. They began as *one flesh* and *one spirit* but end up divided by passing attractions, entering and exiting unions, moving from one household to another, from one country to the next, leaving children scattered everywhere. Many parents and children now live in solitude — rejected, jealous, betrayed, abandoned, unhappy, depressed, and burdened by sadness.

I do not wish to exaggerate, but it is precisely from such breakdowns that delinquency, cruelty, and cynical wickedness arise. Even when the news highlights the presence of a father, he is often humiliated — his degradation synonymous with the suffering of his children. His absence, whether physical or moral, leaves a painful void, creating wounds that fuel deeper dysfunction in family and society.

The mass media, imposing its models and shaping public attitudes, is controlled by economic, ideological, religious, and political forces. It warps the personalities of both its operators and its audience, all while being directed by those who themselves have suffered from the absence of a father or mother. Giorgio Bocca, for instance, notes that those who pull the strings of public life are often politicians who "are orphans and no longer have fathers or mothers who raise them, but are poor straw men chasing the blind symbols of profit and money, accumulating blunders and childish errors."[22]

Many entrusted with education — whether in schools, politics, law enforcement, or even as parents — struggle to provide their children with even the most basic goods, let alone an education that recognizes and safeguards their intrinsic sacredness. Some, rather than nurturing their children, abuse and degrade them, destroying their sense of the sacred, their inner energy, and their ability to enter adulthood with happiness, confidence, and responsibility.

As they raise their children, such parents invent their own *rites of initiation*, but these are not always beneficial. Burdened by confusion and an ongoing sense of frustration, they always find countless ways to avoid their responsibilities — handing over their children's

---

[22] In L'*Espresso*, October 20, 2005, 15.

formation to others, submitting themselves to corrupt knowledge and misguided influences, and in the process, allowing themselves to be enslaved by destructive powers.

Are you saying that the presence of the father is necessary to keep a child from becoming evil?

This is not the place to provide a definitive answer to this question, nor do I claim to be an expert on such matters. What I offer here is simply an attempt to shed a bit of light — perhaps to help parents and their children in some small way.

This brings us to the well-known dilemma: Does the problem begin with the egg or with the hen? In this case, I start with the hen — or rather, the rooster. And I do not place the blame on him.

The absence of the father in the family has many consequences. Among them, daughters who have never known a father's role will struggle in their relationships with their husbands. Sons, lacking a father to discipline them and teach them how to face the world, will be weak as a result.

The sacred father — the true and righteous father — allows his son to seek out his own path, to develop his identity, character, and potential. It is the father's role to guide his son freely, realistically, and with authority. This requires a purposeful and structured pedagogical approach — not one that merely conforms the child to the expectations of culture and society, but one that forms him with a deep awareness of himself, anchoring both his body and soul in reality. In this way, he is initiated and prepared to face the world. A properly understood father-son relationship involves both engagement and detachment. The father loves in a way that allows his son to surrender himself with trust, knowing that his parents take full responsibility for him.

If a son is not equipped to face life and death, he will be in grave trouble, for he will lack the essential tools needed to move forward and complete his existence, whenever that may come. The fear of this possible deficiency gives rise to timidity, indecision, and anxiety — crippling his vital energy and courage. Signs of sadness and inertia will mark his face. He will stop eating, drinking, working, acting, and loving. His life will become agonizing — a state of dying without being able to die, a crucified existence. Without energy or creativity, even vocational training will be of no use, for he will not be an expert in the art of living.

Indeed, when a son shows irresoluteness, indecision, and unfamiliarity with carrying out his most fundamental role — encountering reality and living his existence with courage, dignity, and honor — it is a sign that he was never properly introduced into the art of good living.

In such a condition, sons become weak, heedless, submissive — perpetual dependents, passive to the point of helplessness. Yet within them, something sharpens: the claw of pain, which drives them to compare their lives with the success and moral superiority of those outside the coalition of the weak. At this point, for the sake of survival, they play their last card — that of the victim, weaponizing their own suffering and that of others. They transform their weakness, jealousy, envy, and cynicism into an instrument of power and resentment:

"Let us lie in wait for the righteous man, because he is inconvenient to us," we read in the book of Wisdom. "He calls himself a child of the Lord. ... Let us test him with insult and torture, that we may find out how gentle he is, and make trial of his forbearance. Let us condemn him to a shameful death" (Wis. 2:12, 13, 19–20).

Similarly, in the book of Jeremiah, according to the Latin version, it is written: "Mittamus lignum in panem eius" (Let us hide a sharp piece of wood in the bread that he eats). "Let us destroy the tree with its fruit, let us cut him off from the land of the living, that his name be remembered no more" (Jer. 11:19).

This, in the end, is why we pity the obliged weak — those incapable of ever fully being born, of growing, of confronting life. They are people who cannot stand on their own feet, forever anxious — little chicks pecking timidly at existence, adversity, and death.

Do they lack the lifeblood, the preparation, the teaching, the care, and the love they needed? Yes — because this is a matter of love. The love necessary to be born, to live, and to die. Did they lack a father and a mother? It is likely. If a son has no desire to live, it is not merely because life is difficult, but most often because he was deprived of the sacred, archetypal, and indispensable guidance of parents who would have prepared him with wisdom and love.

What advantages do children of attentive, caring parents have?

In common parlance, people who are *fulfilled* are those who are satiated — not in the sense of mere material satisfaction, but in that they live with the experience and awareness of being loved, recognized, and blessed by their father and mother, the most significant people in their lives. This sense of love and recognition gives rise to an inner happiness that, in turn, leads them to love others and to do good.

The need to *always* feel loved by one's parents is not an infantile regression but, as Cardinal Carlo Maria Martini wrote, "an evocation of the origin, of the womb, of the homeland, of home and the heart where we place all that we are, the face we look to without fear and entrust ourselves to without hesitation in the certainty of being welcomed."

The biblical scholar Bruno Maggioni further explains, "The condition of sonship does not belong to one period of life, but to all one's life. The Bible rightly defines man as a son of man. Man is always a son, desirous of being loved, needing to entrust himself to someone who will accompany him, always seeking a reference point. The Gospel shows its profound humanity when it states that we must become 'like children' to enter the kingdom of heaven. Remaining sons is always the right position of man before God."

The filial attitude that we assume toward our parents is one of generous sharing. The love we have received from them is meant to be extended to others. Charity is needed most of all by those who have never had — or who have been deprived of — a father or mother. Sons who, rather than growing into adulthood, find themselves orphaned are left with fewer defenses and are more vulnerable, even exposed, to evil.

Why put up resistance to evil and not to those who perform it?

The *wrath of God* against the impious is vividly described in the Bible: "a God who has indignation every day" (Ps. 7:11). Even St. Paul, after his conversion, recalls and warns of the *wrath of God*. However, this is not an emotional or irascible state within the Divinity, nor is it a malevolent hatred or the capricious jealousy of the Creator. Rather, it is His resolute reaction to evil, which fully reveals His divine justice.

Paul clarifies that *God's justice* and *justification* correspond to His benevolent and salvific action on behalf of humanity, for God is faithful, merciful, and loving. If those who observe the Law of God, given through Moses, fail to recognize the active love of the Divine Legislator behind it, then for them, the Law has no soul; it becomes nothing more than a heavy burden.

Regarding the expression *resist not evil*, it must be noted that the evangelist Matthew places these words in Jesus' mouth in the context of fulfilling the old divine Law: "You have heard that it was said, 'An eye for an eye and a tooth for a tooth.' But I say to you, Do not resist one who is evil. But if anyone strikes you on the right cheek, turn to him the other also" (Matt. 5:38–39). The phrase *resist not evil* should be understood in the sense of *Do not resist the evil one* — meaning that one must not retaliate against the person committing evil. However, this does not imply acquiescence to the evil itself.

How should we behave with the evil ones, according to the Word of God?

"An eye for an eye and a tooth for a tooth" (Exod. 21:24) expresses the law of retaliation, which was common among the peoples of the Ancient Near East. The Code of Hammurabi, the legal code of the first dynasty of Babylon (18th century B.C.), prescribed that an injury inflicted on another must be repaid in equal measure. It states: "If a man blinds the eye of another, his eye will be blinded" (art. 196); "If a man breaks another man's bone, his bone shall be broken" (art. 197); and "If a man breaks the tooth of another man, his tooth shall be broken" (art. 200).

This principle was later incorporated into the Mosaic Law: "Your eye shall not take compassion: life for life, eye for eye, tooth for tooth, hand for hand, foot for foot, broken bone for broken bone." At the time, this law represented a standard of equity, serving as a deterrent to the excesses of unchecked vengeance.

Alongside this principle — which, in a society with little legal development, effectively codified private revenge — there emerged a tendency to mitigate its severity by substituting pecuniary penalties in place of bodily harm. Gradually, a higher moral standard began to take root in Israel, one that favored non-violence. The righteous man was called to extinguish hatred in his heart toward his brother: "You shall not seek vengeance nor shall you hold a grudge against the son of your people: You shall love your neighbor as yourself."

The forgiveness of the patriarch Joseph toward his brothers is a well-known example. He does not seek vengeance for the evil they did to him but instead interprets his suffering as part of a divine plan that brought good out of evil: "Do not be distressed or angry with yourselves because you sold me here, for God sent me before you to preserve life. For the famine has been in the land these two years, and there are yet five years in which there will be neither plowing nor harvest. And God has sent me before you to preserve for you a remnant on earth, and to keep alive for you many survivors. So it was not you who sent me here, but God" (Gen. 45:5–8).

Similarly, David does not take revenge on Saul, who persecutes him, even when given the opportunity to kill him.

Later, in the Psalms, the book of Job, and the prophetic writings — especially Jeremiah — the reason why the righteous man renounces vengeance becomes explicit. He is invited to place his cause and his trust in God's hands, refusing to take revenge and instead relying on divine justice. God is the supreme Judge, the only One who scrutinizes the hearts of both individuals and entire peoples, rewarding or punishing them according to their deeds.

In the book of the Prophet Isaiah, we find the mysterious figure of the "Servant of Yahweh." In Jewish tradition — attested in the Targum and ancient rabbinical exegesis — this Servant is identified with the liberating Messiah. In Christian tradition, He is recognized as Jesus Christ, based on the numerous and explicit references in the New Testament. The trial endured by the Servant, "so marred" (Isa. 52:14), and His final vindication prefigure the Passion and glorification of Christ Jesus: suffering, beaten, crucified, buried, and then resurrected. "I gave My back to the smiters, and My cheeks to those who pulled out My beard; I hid not My face from shame and spitting. For the Lord God helps Me; therefore I have not been confounded" (Isa. 50:6–7). This is how the incarnate divine Son behaved.

This glorious Messiah — the most beautiful among the sons of men — was struck with brutal physical violence that disfigured His human form. He was humiliated and scorned, tested in both body and soul. His sufferings unfolded progressively: He was beaten, His beard was pulled out, He was insulted and spat upon — one of the gravest affronts in Near Eastern culture. The account presents a man who is utterly ruined, stripped not only of dignity but of any semblance of beauty or attraction. He was reduced to a mere shadow of a human being. And yet, from this state, He would be liberated.

What is new and striking about the account of the Servant is that He not only refuses to resist His tormentors but even submits to their insults, making Himself almost insensible to them. He meekly accepts the suffering inflicted upon Him: "He was oppressed and was afflicted, yet He opened not His mouth" (Isa. 53:7). The reason is clear: The One who watches over Him and aids Him is God Himself. This trial is permitted by God to bring Him to maturity, making Him worthy of His great mission. And so, after His profound suffering, this "Man of Sorrows and acquainted with grief" (Isa. 53:3) will regain His appearance, return to the light, and rejoice — satisfied in His endurance and in the help of God, which enabled Him to triumph over adversity.

Even in the Old Testament, however, the ideal of replacing vengeance with love often remained difficult to achieve in practice. The so-called *imprecatory* Psalms bear witness to this struggle. It would ultimately be the task of the New Testament to reveal the necessity of not resisting the evil one.

How does Jesus treat evil people?

The Word of God provides, above all, a pedagogical interpretation of the painful story of Christ Jesus, the Son. How could the Father have allowed the man Christ Jesus to be crucified and accept death on the Cross? It must be understood that this fate was not unique to Him. Consider Spartacus and his many companions, impaled along the Appian Way. The difference, however, lies in the fact that the Crucified One did not rebel against the Father, nor did He resist those who crucified Him.

Undoubtedly, the Father did not impose the Cross upon Jesus lightly. Rather, He prepared Him, guided Him, and strengthened Him for that moment, granting Him above all the awareness that He was not merely a servant but a Son: "It is too light a thing that You should be My servant" (Isa. 49:6); "You are My Son, today I have begotten You" (Ps. 2:7).

He is the Son, not a servant disciplined like one under subjection. As we read in the book of Proverbs, and as it is reiterated in the Letter to the Hebrews: "My son, do not regard lightly the discipline of the Lord, nor lose courage when you are punished by Him. For the Lord disciplines him whom He loves and chastises every son whom He receives. … For the moment all discipline seems painful rather than pleasant; later it yields the peaceful fruit of righteousness to those who have been trained by it" (Heb. 12:5, 11).

Christ Jesus is the beloved Son of the Father. And so, He is not saddened by the discipline He receives. Rather, His identity as Son and His intimacy with the Father fill Him with joy, to the point of fully embracing the Father's plan. Through the Son-made-man, the Father offers the gift of loving adoption to all who recognize their need to be loved and made whole.

Would you like to say more about this divine pedagogy?

The Father's pedagogy, as applied to the man Jesus, is revealed in the Gospels. It is for an essentially *disciplinary* purpose that the divine Spirit leads Jesus Christ to relive the very experience of the ancient Jewish people in their journey through the desert. He is baptized, passing through the waters of the Jordan, just as the people of Israel once crossed the same river. He submits to trials and temptations in the desert, entering into the experience and memory of exile — of being strangers, servants, and wanderers. He then enters the promised land alongside the people of the New Covenant.

Yet His coming is no longer proclaimed as the *day of vengeance* but as the day of salvation. He partakes of the bread and wine of this land, now transformed into His body and blood. He turns His face *resolutely* toward adversity, like a valiant warrior, *tried in affliction,* bearing *our infirmities* and carrying *our afflictions.*

How does he manifest the state of an "adult" Son?

While the Master rejects evil, He Himself is rejected and cast out by the religious spirit of His people. Though He is the Son, He finds no welcome; He is driven from the vineyard — from the land, so to speak, promised and given to Israel — and is put to death outside the city, at the hands of both His own countrymen and the pagans. He is condemned by the world: "the world knew Him not" (John 1:10); "the darkness has not overcome Him" (John 1:5). Even His own disciples abandoned Him: "His own people received Him not" (John 1:11), and so He was compelled to offer salvation elsewhere. Indeed, it was a pagan centurion who, standing at the foot of the Cross, recognized Him: "Truly this man was the Son of God!" (Mark 15:39).

What is superhuman in Jesus Christ is the fact that "when He was reviled, He did not revile in return; when He suffered, He did not threaten; but He trusted to Him who judges justly" (1 Pet. 2:23). For those who crucified Him, He offers a prayer: "Father, forgive them, for they know not what they do" (Luke 23:34), because "they do not know Him who sent Me" (John 15:21), namely, the Father.

If, then, the Son does not resist the evil one, but instead conquers the cynicism of men and death through the very Cross imposed upon Him by the wicked, it is because, throughout His earthly life — especially while hanging from the Cross — He knows with absolute certainty that the Father is present, assuring Him:

✠ "I have taken You by the hand. … Fear not, for I have redeemed You; I have called You by name, You are Mine. When You pass through the waters, I will be with You; and through the rivers, they shall not overwhelm You; when You walk through fire, You shall not be burned, and the flame shall not consume You. … Because You are precious in My eyes, and honored, and I love You" (Isa. 42:6; 43:1–4).

✠ "I will never fail You nor forsake You" (Heb. 13:5).

✠ Convinced that He has not been abandoned by the Father, He surrenders Himself completely into His hands:

✠ "He who sent Me is with Me; He has not left Me alone" (John 8:29).

✠ "My recompense is with God" (Isa. 49:4).

✠ "For the Lord God helps Me" (Isa. 50:7).

✠ "Father, I thank Thee that Thou hast heard Me. I knew that Thou hearest Me always" (John 11:41–42).

✠ "Father, into Thy hands I commit My spirit!" (Luke 23:46).

I repeat: The *joy* of the Son is in knowing He is loved by the Father, precisely in His suffering on the Cross. The *joy* of the Father is in seeing before His own eyes the Son *perfected* — a man who faces death with full maturity:

"Behold My servant, whom I uphold, My chosen, in whom My soul delights" (Isa. 42:1); He "will not fail or be discouraged" (Isa. 42:4).

How does the understanding between Father and Son arise and mature?

The presence of the Father was not a sudden event for Jesus, nor an unexpected apparition or an unhoped-for intervention. Christ, who is *in the bosom of the Father*, had always recognized the Father, knowing with certainty that He would be heard and never abandoned. How could He have felt the Father's closeness in the terrible moment of His death had He not already experienced the tenderness of the One in whose bosom He dwelled? Jesus knows the Father because He comes from Him. He trusts Him because He knows that He exists and has lived in His presence for all eternity. He feels the absolute assurance of the Father's tenderness.

Thus, God sent His Son, Jesus Christ, into the world. His death on the Cross reveals and brings to completion the full extent of human wickedness. At the same time, it manifests how God is divinely just, good, and tender toward the sinner, while He remains strong, terrible, and implacable against evil. The Cross that fell upon Jesus — treating Him as sin on our behalf — is the radical *no* to evil and the most loving *yes* to the sinner. For this reason, on the Cross, the word spoken by Isaiah was fulfilled: "Righteousness and peace have kissed" (Ps. 85:10). Through the blood poured out on the Cross, humanity remains, even now, *very good*, for the justice of God was poured out upon the One who represented and renewed it.

The Son Jesus, disfigured yet meek before evil, stands in solidarity with all who suffer physical and psychological violence. This suffering tempts us to seek vengeance, to return blow for blow, rather than to bear it with meekness.

Yet, the call not to resist the evil one — to conquer evil with good — does not negate the rightful exercise of justice on earth, nor does it undermine the established juridical order.

How should we Christians behave with those who are evil?

Regarding non-resistance to the evil one, Jesus teaches that we are not the ones to decide who our neighbor is — whom we must understand, forgive, and love as ourselves. In the parable of the Good Samaritan, we learn that our neighbor is every person whom God places in our path, whether good, bad, or even an enemy.

St. Paul, convinced that Christians are the blessed beneficiaries of God's grace, exhorts us to act in an unrelentingly constructive manner, striving to reflect as closely as possible the beneficent and blessing action of the Lord. He presents to the Christians of Corinth the magnificent *Hymn to Love*, emphasizing that love "does not rejoice at wrong [suffered]" (1 Cor. 13:5). Writing to the Christians in Rome, he affirms that love does no harm to its neighbor, declaring that "the fullness of the law is love" (see Rom. 13:1–13). To the Thessalonians, he repeats: "See that none of you repays evil for evil, but always seek to do good to one another and to all" (1 Thess. 5:15).

He exhorts the Christian community to be a witness to others, like "a city on a hill" (Matt. 5:14), and to "repay no one evil for evil" (Rom. 12:17), renouncing vengeance and instead conquering evil with good.

How can we love our enemies?

We may certainly be disturbed by injustice. Yet even in such circumstances, the Christian must remain charitable, overflowing with God's free gift, without harboring a spirit of vengeance for wrongs suffered. One must not seek retribution, attempting to restore a disturbed balance by one's own hand. If evil persists, leave it to God to re-establish equilibrium, so that those who have committed evil may repent. The Christian must adopt an attitude of meekness — always and toward everyone, even those outside ecclesial communion.

I recall a wise teaching from Blessed Fr. Giacomo Alberione (1884–1971)[23] regarding the so-called enemies of the Church. "There are the enemies of the Church, and by enemies I mean those who hate us. Oh, we must pray for them as well," he exhorted. "Jesus prayed for those who crucified Him, eh! Pray for them, that the Lord might illuminate them and attract them to Himself with His grace. Always treat them well, yes, treat them with respect, but do not condone their errors. However, while loving them and praying for them, desire eternal life for them; do not acquiesce to their errors, do not walk with them in their life that is perhaps not good. Have compassion on them and pray all the more as you see they lack interior light and do not yet possess grace."

Concretely, what are the "modalities" for resisting not evil and one's enemies?

In martial arts, aggression and blows from an adversary are not always met with direct force but are often neutralized by redirecting their energy, allowing it to dissipate. In a similar way, rather than relying on techniques of resistance, the Christian allows himself to be pierced by aggression and insult, knowing in whom he has placed his hope (see 2 Tim. 1:12).

How can one overcome the natural human instinct to react to offense or seek vengeance? Here are some reasons:

---

[23]   Founder of the Society of St. Paul, to which Fr. Amorth and Fr. De Simone belong, as well as nine other religious institutes that compose the Pauline Family that he founded.

✠ **Because the evil others do to us does not "entirely" destroy us, and we can endure it without seeking vengeance.** If we have experienced the love of God the Father as revealed in His Son Jesus — *with His stripes we are healed* (Isa. 53:5) — we know that nothing can separate us from this love. As Jesus Himself tells us, we are not to fear those who can kill the body, but rather the one who can kill the soul. We have been assured that not even a hair of our head will be lost, so we can confidently surrender ourselves to the Father.

✠ **Because, as St. Paul says, we ourselves struggle to do good, often doing the very evil we wish to avoid.** "I do not do what I want, but I do the very thing I hate" (Rom. 7:15), Paul admits, disoriented because he does not understand his own actions. He recognizes a deep dysfunction within himself: Though he desires what is good, human weakness leads him astray. In all of us, there exists God's law, which directs the inner person toward the good, but also another law, working in our members, that enslaves us to sin. "Wretched man that I am!" he exclaims in despair, "Who will deliver me from this body of death?" (Rom. 7:24). Why, then, should we harass those already burdened by their own failings? Only God is Judge, for He alone sees the heart.

✠ **Because our true adversary is not the one who offends us.** Our struggle is not against flesh and blood but against the evil spirits that dwell in the darkness of this world. That is why we arm ourselves with the light of Christ to combat and resist evil — while at the same time, we are called not to resist those who do us harm. Jesus Himself resisted the temptation of Satan and cast demons out of the possessed. He always bore witness to the Truth and firmly opposed the *righteousness* of the Pharisees, yet He did not resist evil men, allowing

Himself instead to be killed by them. From the Cross, He even forgave His executioners: "Father, forgive them, for they know not what they do" (Luke 23:34).

✠ **Because those who do us wrong are already "dead" in their wickedness.** There is no need to rage against them, for their own evil is already their recompense. St. Paul writes to the Christians in Rome, "There will be tribulation and distress for every human being who does evil" (Rom. 2:9). Those who wrong us have not known the Father, they do not feel loved, and they are deeply troubled. Jesus explained to His disciples, "All this they will do to you on My account, because they do not know Him who sent Me" (John 15:21). How, then, can a Christian be angry with those who are so lost? Instead, he overflows with love for them. He knows that those who insult and harm him do so because they lack love and are tormented. This is the profound reason why Jesus exhorts us to turn the other cheek. By doing so, we overcome evil with good, revealing to our persecutors that they do not face an enemy, but someone who loves them — because he has first encountered the love of God the Father, Son, and Holy Spirit. As members of the Church, we are on the list of those who have been loved and forgiven. We are therefore called to forgive, so that others too may experience the unconditional love of God and find themselves on that same list. All the saints, and above all the martyrs, have given this witness — first among them, St. Stephen, who died praying that God would not hold his executioners guilty.

✠ **Because only in this way will we have peace.** "Blessed are the meek, for they shall inherit the earth" (Matt. 5:5) — a promise given not to those who seek vengeance, but to those who renounce it. Vengeance does not break the chain of evil; it perpetuates and worsens it. How much better it is to delight in what is good rather than to be consumed by hatred and intrigue, which rob us of peace!

✠ **Because in this way alone do we reflect the image and likeness of God.** As St. Columban writes, "A great dignity is granted man from this resemblance with God, as long as he knows how to preserve it. We are not, therefore, painters of an image different from this one. Whoever is violent, vindictive, quick to wrath, and proud paints in himself the image of a tyrant." We are also sons of the heavenly Father, who makes His sun rise and sends rain on both the just and the unjust, the good and the evil alike. Jesus went before us, living as true Man, showing divine charity as the foundation of all human thought and action.

For this reason, we should not be discouraged, asking ourselves, *Will we ever be perfect? Will we ever attain a love like that of Jesus, the saints, and the martyrs?* Let us not lose heart. Christians are not only those who have already reached sanctity and perfection, but also those who are on the path, those who fall and rise again. Though it is difficult to live according to the Word of God, what matters is that it always remains the *motor* that propels us toward the goal. We can always draw upon divine grace, the Eucharist, Confession, and the other Sacraments to acquire "the ability to bear offenses and to find patience under trial."

As we read in *The Imitation of Christ*: "The truly patient man is the one who does not concern himself with who tests him — whether it be his superior, a peer, or a subordinate; whether a good man or a saint, or a wicked man of no merit. The truly patient man, no matter who or how often he is contradicted, accepts all things with a grateful soul from the hand of God. In fact, he considers it a great advantage, because nothing — however small — if endured for love of God, will go without recompense."

Thus, all the devilish schemes of demons and wicked men, who seek to subjugate us, lose their power. Having experienced the love of the Father, we surrender ourselves entirely to Him, like "a child quieted at its mother's breast" (Ps. 131:2), certain that no force of evil can separate us from the love of Christ.

Is the Christian experience still valid as a remedy to the prevailing evil in the world?

Authentic Christian experience is not only a remedy for evils of every kind but also a powerful means of prevention. Christianity elevates and exalts values that promote the person, the good, and reality itself. To these, I would add: interiority, harmony between reason and faith, and openness to transcendence — not as an escape, but as the continual possibility of authentically experiencing God without mystification. To return to these values is to reaffirm principles that hold universal validity.

The authentic Christian participates in our shared humanity even before professing his religious creed. He perceives the transcendence of God and, with it, the theology of creation — no longer separating material and spiritual processes, nor succumbing to superstitions that risk degenerating into crude revivals and imitations of paganism.

To recognize God as Creator means not only acknowledging His work within creation but also embracing one's own calling to enter into communion with Him as both a witness and a direct collaborator on earth. Becoming aware of this responsibility grants energy and talent to transform the reality in which one lives — actively working for the good despite the encroachment of evil in society, so that it may truly conform to God's plan in Christ.

The Christian bears witness through his own experience, contributing to the renewal of civil society, family life, and the workplace, permeating every aspect of reality with his presence, professional competence, friendships, and solidarity.

Throughout history, Christians have defended the autonomy of created realities, consistently engaging with the world and assuming personal responsibility for society and the environment. They have upheld the rule of law and fostered respect for nature, work, culture, and science — all illuminated by Christian hope.

As new discoveries have challenged the traditional theocentric and anthropocentric interpretations of creation, offering surprising insights into both the macrocosm and microcosm, each scientific advancement has prompted Christians to reformulate and reaffirm their faith in the Creator. They have done so while respecting scientific knowledge, through which they taste and recognize the living wisdom of God.

Even today, Christians confront ideologies that seek to divide body and soul, creature and Creator, Church and world, sacred and profane. Equipped with the armor of God, they stand firm in the freedom to speak out against evil and against every seed of discord among individuals and nations.

Are we Christians truly a "mirror" of the loving face of Christ?

People can see the loving face of God in authentic Christians only if we, as Christians, are first aware that we ourselves are made in His image and likeness. St. Paul writes to the Christians in Corinth, "And we all, with unveiled faces, beholding the glory of the Lord, are being changed into His likeness from one degree of glory to another; for this comes from the Lord who is the Spirit" (2 Cor. 3:18).

The divine presence is not revealed solely in the beauty of Eastern icons, the snow-covered landscapes of the Dolomites, or the transparent innocence in the eyes of a child. The face of the Lord is made visible in the very identity He has restored to us.

Having tasted the sweetness of the divine gift — the deeply gratifying and joyous experience of God the Father, Son, and Holy Spirit — the Christian, knowing himself as a beloved and loveable son, instills this gift into his testimony. The divine free gift shines forth, overflows, and is poured out in his life. Herein lies the capacity for doing good: We first receive it from the One who alone can guarantee the gift, filling our hearts, even as they hold within them so many contradictions — limits and aspirations, attractions and weaknesses, desires and dissatisfactions, crucifixion and Resurrection, death and life.

Our God captivates us when He visits us, revealing Himself in our gestures of fortitude, integrity, and charity — standing in defiance of all the empty promises of evil that seek to subjugate us. Those who glimpse our human face and recognize our generosity toward the *least* are drawn to God, who is the fundamental source of our Christian life and actions.

We do not see humanity as hopelessly lost or condemned. Rather, we stir ourselves not to neglect others but to extend our aid, bearing witness through our lives and reflecting the gentleness of the Father so that joy and true peace may return to those who have lost them. As human beings and as Christians, we become stewards of goodness, sharing freely and without hesitation all that has been given to us — our very breath and life, food and clothing, affection and material goods — so that every person may have what is necessary for life. We do this in full liberty, without restriction, condition, or limit of any kind.

In the end, we recognize Christ crucified in our suffering neighbor, and we reveal His Resurrection through our works and through our very faces. This is the true way of raising others from every kind of tomb.

Dear father, you are offering a utopian vision!

Who, then, is truly better off — the one who does good or the one who does evil? Let the millionaire come and answer me, with his ulcerated stomach, worn down by the endless worries of amassing wealth. Let the many missionaries come and speak — those who have dedicated their entire lives to doing good, promoting the well-being of others, advancing civilization, upholding human rights, fostering education, and defending human dignity. These are the ones who bear witness to the Source of all goodness, which is God.

We can take up the words of the divine Master: "If anyone strikes you on the right cheek, turn to him the other also" (Matt. 5:39). And I would add: To strike the right cheek of the person in front of me with my right hand, I cannot slap him directly — I must strike with the back of my hand. This kind of blow was, and still is, the greatest form of humiliation (once, men would strike each other with gloves as a similar insult). And yet, even in such an affront, I turn to him the other cheek. Why? Because I lose nothing — I am *sated* by the One who loves me with an eternal love and has given Himself for me.

And I say more: By responding in this way, I not only love and forgive the one who strikes me, but I *surprise* him. I confound him to the point that he is drawn to me. And once I have reached this moment, he can only seek to understand the profound reason why I have offered him my other cheek. He realizes it is not cowardice, self-abasement, or pusillanimity, but the strength that comes from being *sated* — even to the point of *indigestion* — with the divine free gift. And so he stops and wonders, saying along with St. Augustine, "Why so much love for him and not for me?" In this way, he too is moved to surrender to the love of the good God.

This approach — this refusal to resist the evil one — is always a winning card. But to behave in such a way, I must first remember that I am *sated*, not starving, for divine love.

Tranquil and smiling toward all, Fr. Gabriele was nevertheless determined and stern with the evil one.

CHAPTER NINE

"What Evil Can They Do to Me?"[24]

"If the Lord is as powerful as I know and can see he is; if the demons are only slaves to him, as faith does not allow me to doubt, what evil can they do to me if I am the daughter of this King and Lord?"[25]

Why do many people "emphasize" the devil?

A certain literary and artistic culture of the past has mythologized, mystified, and distorted the figure of the devil — either to obscure his true identity and nature or to exalt his presence and activity. Authors such as Julian the Apostate (*The Restoration of Paganism*), John Milton (*Paradise Lost*), Johann Wolfgang von Goethe (*Faust*), Friedrich Nietzsche (*Thus Spoke Zarathustra*), Giosuè Carducci (*Hymn to Satan*), and Mario Rapisardi (*Lucifer*) all expressed sympathy for a modern, "innovative" Satan, intending to restore ancient paganism as a form of rebellion, transgression, or rejection of Christianity.

No one disputes that the classical Greco-Roman age has its merits in the realm of humanistic and cultural achievements, despite its pagan foundations. Nevertheless, orthodox Christianity is incomparably more worthy. The medieval English philosopher, teacher, and theologian Alcuin of York collected, interpreted,

---

24 Teresa of Avila, *Life*, XXV, 19–22.
25 Ibid.

translated, and transmitted classical Greek and Roman works in response to the intellectual needs of his time. His efforts contributed to the preservation and renewal of the treasures of ancient knowledge, which had long been hidden to protect them from barbarian invasions. Through his rhetorical, pedagogical, and philosophical writings, Alcuin played a crucial role in safeguarding and promoting both classical and medieval learning.

In Italy today, there is considerable interest in classical literature and the histories of Egyptian, Greek, and Roman civilizations. However, much of this attention is directed toward reviving a "reconsidered" paganism, seeking to reintroduce it *in toto* as an alternative to Christian culture.

Such proposals remain far removed from the reality of evil and the figure of the devil as presented in Sacred Scripture. They seek to deny the existence of the devil, yet in doing so, they implicitly acknowledge him — attempting instead to obscure the undeniable traces of his destructive influence throughout history and in the dark events of our own time. The exorcist, however, sees the devil with his own eyes.

As a result, many people are left disoriented, sustained by an assertive elite in power — bolstered by practical atheism and Freemasonry — which fuels war, injustice, corruption, and ecological devastation in a world that we are called to safeguard and cultivate for the good. The modern emphasis on personal liberty as an end in itself is diabolical, lacking any proper formation in the responsible and constructive use of freedom. This moral void leads to the degradation of human dignity and worth, leaving individuals vulnerable to knowledge and powers that often oppress the weak and defenseless.

The many faces of the devil — manifest in both ideology and action — only further confuse society, all while avoiding direct mention of the dark angel himself. Those who seek to expose his intrigues are often silenced or ridiculed.

The renowned theologian Karl Rahner once stated that he would "not exaggerate" the role of the devil because "in the face of the seriousness of salvation history, it would be a sign of scarce theological precision to see in the devil and in demons spirits or ghosts that prowl about the world. Much more precise is to hold that these are worldly powers (war, tyranny, etc.), since this world is man's repudiation of God and temptation to evil." In essence, Rahner argues that rather than fixating on the devil as a spectral entity, we must understand how to put an end to evil and commit ourselves to the pursuit of the good — without excuses, false narratives, or evasions.

In your opinion, what contribution does atheistic Freemasonry offer to such manipulations?

In essence, Freemasonry — whose true nature and aims are difficult to define precisely because of its *secret* character — is not explicitly tied to either the experience of God or the figure of the devil. Rather, it is concerned with the *idea* of God, religion, the temple, and, in particular, the cult of Lucifer. Fundamentally, it presents itself as *the* Religion, complete with initiation rites, hierarchical degrees, rituals, and lodges.

One of Freemasonry's defining statements is articulated by Joseph Fort Newton, one of its most influential ideologues and advocates: "Since the human soul is akin to God and is endowed with powers on which no one can place limits, it is *de facto*, and must be *de jure*, free. Thus, according to the logic of its philosophy as well as the inspiration of faith, Freemasonry was led to present in history its questions about the freedom of conscience, the freedom of the intellect, and the rights of all men to rise up without fear, all equal before God and the law, each ready to respect the rights of his peers."

This *honest* definition and proposal of freedom — as a value and a right grounded in the *affinity* between the human soul and God — is an attempt to establish and justify an absolute and unambiguous notion of liberty. Indeed, freedom is one of Freemasonry's central goals. However, Newton's claim that "no one can place limits" on human freedom is only true if "no one" refers strictly to human beings. If, however, this statement is taken to include God, then it is false — for the only One who can rightly limit the creature is the Creator, God, the Absolute.

The fact remains that many of the "powerful" and "wise" of the world are affiliated with Freemasonry. Observing the current state of world affairs, it would be delusional to believe that Freemasonry is truly concerned with liberating humanity. Power and knowledge largely dictate the course of history, and rather than serving human freedom, they are often directed toward ruin, as those who wield them attempt to substitute themselves for God. We know well the fate of the angel of light who sought to replace God — only to become an angel of darkness, working in secret like Freemasonry, the mafia, the Camorra, and the 'Ndrangheta.

In your opinion, does a particularly Masonic nation exist, in the sense that it defends, promotes, and carries out its ideology?

I do not believe I can respond adequately; I am not capable of that. Rather than identifying a single nation, I think I can outline the reasons why any nation might fall prey to an ideology that is, at the very least, inhumane. No one will ever be able to displace God — I am certain of that. But if people do not rediscover a *taste* for the good, without falling into the delusions and deceptions of evil and its proponents, they will continue to dismantle the human person — both individually and collectively.

When the train of ideology arrives, there will always be those willing to climb aboard. Throughout the world, many are persuaded toward evil, anger, discord, and discontent. In their frustration, they seek a scapegoat — be it God, Christianity, or the Church. Others shift their allegiance to a form of neo-pagan naturalism, whether gnostic, Masonic, or atheistic. This seems to be the trajectory of the most de-Christianized nations, where moral relativism is promoted alongside abortion, homosexual marriage, and — more broadly — the pagan and gnostic spirit, which does little to advance the dignity of man.

Many, like the American writer Dan Brown, consider this development positive, as it provides justification for marginalizing Christianity from modern social and political life. However, during his 2008 visit to the United States, Benedict XVI reminded the world that "the principles that govern social and political life" must be "intimately tied to the moral order, based on the lordship of God the Creator." He clarified that this is the God "of biblical faith" — which is to say, the Christian God.

Furthermore, there is a deliberate effort to reject the Christian culture that developed historically in Europe — many considering it to be *surpassed*. But surpassed by what? Not by a more refined civilization, but by the rise of American, Chinese, and Arabian capitalism — none of which has retained the slightest respect for either the human person or the Creator.

Father Gabriele, are you afraid of the devil and of this diabolical network which is like a "long arm"?

That Satan's fury is unleashed? Fear? God is and remains with me. The evil one exists, but he fears our Lord. True faith and prayer — these are formidable bastions against the devil.

It is well known that the devil is a spirit, meaning he is not bound by a body and is therefore superior to the exorcist in both intelligence and strength. However, the exorcist is not a fearful man — nor does he seek to challenge the devil, for to do so would be like playing with fire. In any case, he has no need to. He knows from direct experience that the devil will attack him, for as a human being created in the image and likeness of God, as a Christian, a priest, and above all an exorcist, he is guaranteed divine protection and is fully equipped to defend himself.

Even the ordinary Christian, living in God's grace and praying fervently, is strong enough to face the devil. As has been said, the devil does not have the power to take a person's soul; he may cause physical harm, but even then, nothing truly grave.

Both the exorcist and the baptized Christian are secure insofar as they remain aware that they are loved by God the Father, Son, and Holy Spirit, and are protected by the Blessed Virgin Mary, the angels, and the saints. They stand on the side of the Stronger One — the One who is infinitely more powerful and infinitely more attractive.

God grants them all the grace they need to confront and overcome the devil. To his threats, anyone can respond with confidence: "I am wrapped in Our Lady's mantle — what can you do to me? I have the Archangel Michael on my side — try fighting him! My guardian angel watches over me, keeping me from harm — you have no power here."

In her autobiography, St. Teresa of Avila recounts: "If the Lord is as powerful as I know and see He is; if the demons are only slaves to Him, as faith does not allow me to doubt, what evil can they do to me if I am the daughter of this King and Lord? ... And it seems they truly fear me, for I remained at peace in their presence. Since then, those anxieties no longer disturb me, nor am I afraid of demons, because when they appeared to me ... not only was I not afraid, but it seemed they were afraid of me."[26]

---

[26] Ibid.

Who is an exorcist?

First, a brief premise. When it comes to deviousness, the exorcist may, in some ways, understand more than the devil himself. Though far less intelligent than the evil one, he knows — both personally and through experience — how the devil operates. Every priest should possess at least a basic familiarity with these realities to discern whether a person requires the attention of an exorcist. The exorcist's apostolate is among those who suffer terribly — often misunderstood by their families, their doctors, and at times even their parish priests.

To be effective in his ministry and strike at the heart of evil, the exorcist must bear witness to Christian fortitude and hope, which sustain us against every darkness. He remains faithful to the daily celebration of Mass, the Liturgy of the Hours, prayers to the Mother of God, the Archangel Michael, and his personal patron saint. He continually meditates on the Word of God, particularly the readings of the day, the New Testament, and, in a special way, the Prologue of the Gospel of John (1:1–18), the Christological hymns that open the letters to the Ephesians (1:3–14) and Colossians (1:15–20), as well as the second chapter of Philippians (2:6–11).

In these passages, Christ Jesus is made manifest with unmistakable clarity — He who is the beginning, the center, and the end of the created universe, the One who gathers all things to Himself: those in heaven (the angels) and those on earth (all living and inanimate beings).

Are people more confident in the good or more terrorized by evil?

In my opinion people are indifferent, more than anything.

In traditional peasant culture, when a child asked his father who made the heavens, the trees, the flowers, or the animals, he would receive only one answer: "My child, God made all this." Today, when a child caught in the midst of city traffic asks, "Papa, who made the cars?" he hears a very different response: "Fiat did," or "Mercedes," or "Lancia," or the name of some other manufacturer. Progress seeks to replace the Creator with the builders of cars, space shuttles, jumbo jets, and other marvels of human engineering. Giosuè Carducci even went so far as to associate the steam locomotive with Satan himself.

This reveals a deeper truth: When signs of a reality are absent, people come to consider that reality itself absent — or even nonexistent. Yet many, even when deprived of ultimate answers, still feel a deep nostalgia for the good, for God, for a spirituality that allows them to perceive traces of the divine. Often, people are calmed when they enter into a space of goodness and become aware of the sacred. By *space*, I mean not only a physical place but the proposal, the presence, the visibility, the action, and the experience of God in the most tangible sense possible.

For example, when someone meets a priest and instinctively feels at ease, it is because they sense, in some way, that they are touching the divine made manifest in him. This alone is already a great consolation, especially in an age when it has become so difficult to detect and discern the signs of God's presence and action. For this reason, when I encounter people afflicted by malevolent forces, my first effort is not to identify the tracks of the devil, but to look for the traces of the Crucified One in them.

Why do people consider the devil to be so powerful?

Once upon a time, this terrifying subject was not regarded with the same dread that it inspires today. In Greco-Roman religion, a *daimon* (demon) was considered little more than a spirit — a harmless idol, a simple intermediary between men and the gods. Far greater importance was placed on divinity, the efficacy of goodness, and the human capacity to face and overcome all forms of adversity.

Over time, however, as interest in the good waned and evil became increasingly mythologized — with its entire infernal host of demons and devils — the spirit in rebellion against God took on a distinct and fully negative identity, set in absolute opposition to the good.

What advice can we give to those who, on the other hand, are terrorized by the mere idea of the existence of the devil?

Whereas the authentic Christian understands the devil within the limits set by Sacred Scripture and turns instead to the loving presence of God — made tangible in Christ Jesus, the Eucharist, the saints, and the pure spirits (to name just a few holy realities) — many people imagine themselves to be under the sway of all kinds of evil spirits, subject to dark powers from which they desperately seek protection.

At times, yes, the devil is at work — but not always. It is not enough to assume that certain evils are caused by him; there must be proof. While it is true that the evil one operates in the world, perhaps only indirectly, other forces may be at work long before him. We will examine some of these.

When professional expertise, established disciplines, and therapeutic interventions of a psychosomatic nature fail to provide adequate answers or solutions, people often turn elsewhere. They seek help from healers, clairvoyants, card readers, and gurus of every kind — wandering into the tangled jungle of the magical arts. Yet this retreat into the occult is not only insufficient and ineffective; it is also harmful. The real damage lies in the conviction that their suffering stems from demonic forces or, at the very least, from agents beyond human control.

In the end, when all else fails, they turn as a last resort to an exorcist — who then often discovers that the true causes of their affliction lie elsewhere.

What are those causes, for example?

The origin of certain evils or phenomena often lies within the natural order. The various problems, signs, and symptoms observed in some individuals almost always point to physical causes, psychological disorders, or relational conflicts. True cases of demonic possession are quite rare, whereas unhappy people are abundant. If the root of a person's suffering is psychiatric in nature, for example, this will become evident over time through repeated encounters and careful observation.

A report published on page 51 of *Il Mattino* on July 23, 2010, noted that Fr. Pasquale Puca, a Jesuit from the Gesù Nuovo community in Naples, stated that he had encountered approximately five thousand people in his role as an exorcist. "Among all these cases," he explained, "the vast majority were related to psychological disturbances, inner afflictions, or episodes of depression. Only ten individuals truly required greater attention, and even today, some of their cases remain unresolved. Of those ten, only three exhibited particularly violent behavior."

What types of people come to an exorcist?

In responding to you here, my intention is to enlighten ordinary Christians so that they may better recognize and counter the reality of evil and the one who embodies it in this world. For this reason, I will not go into too much detail regarding the ministry of the exorcist.

In general, those who seek out an exorcist have already exhausted other options. Almost always — except in very rare cases — they have first consulted doctors and attempted every available treatment. Unfortunately, many also turn to magicians and occult practitioners along the way. Only after all else has failed do they finally arrive at the exorcist's door.

What are the sufferings that overburden these people?

Oh, all kinds of suffering — both physical and psychological distress. Above all, I encounter people who are depressed, frightened, and at times even terrified. Depression is the most frequent symptom I come across. In such cases, as a priest — not a doctor or psychologist — I always advise them to seek the help of a specialist. Nevertheless, I listen to everyone, for simply being heard is a kind of therapy that benefits all who are suffering.

Yes, this is precisely the case: The exorcist encounters people burdened with suffering, depression, and anxiety. Some recount disasters and terrible events in their lives, emphasizing the darkest aspects of their experience and blaming themselves for their afflictions. We all know that anxiety, for instance, often arises from a lack of true self-understanding, leading a person to insecurity, hesitation, and fear when faced with the realities of life.

I would like to dwell for a moment on a widespread yet imaginary pathology. In many cases, people fall under the power of suggestion and fear, which cast shadows in their minds. Highly impressionable individuals, scrupulous consciences, and those traumatized by painful experiences — exhausted by long periods of suffering — stimulate their own imaginations, which then become a decisive factor in evading the real causes of their distress, hastily attributing their afflictions to the devil.

Let me explain. Some people perceive their experiences as part of an overarching pattern of misfortune. They first attempt to rationalize what is happening, analyzing, modifying, exaggerating, and illuminating every possible explanation. If they fail to make sense of it, they begin to fantasize, seeing themselves as victims of unrelenting bad luck. Their fears are then projected onto non-existent entities or imagined figures, which they come to believe are responsible for their misfortunes. Eventually, they turn to an exorcist, convinced that the root of their suffering must be the direct interference of the devil.

Demonic influence, therefore, can easily be confused with psychological disturbances.

In complex cases, diagnosis requires an interdisciplinary approach. The exorcist must hold doctors and psychiatrists in high regard, recognizing the valuable contributions they provide without prejudice. He may know many professionals in these fields. He intervenes directly only when physical ailments and psychological disorders — though properly diagnosed — prove to be untreatable.

Has anyone ever confided to being so "wicked" that they are afraid of themselves?

Certainly, evil exists within us as well, along with our inability to fight it or overcome it completely. After all, who does not feel, at some point, that their will is weak in the face of evil? Yet, if a person were to be afraid of himself, that would be a real problem — hellish, even. Imagine waking up in the morning, looking at yourself in the mirror, turning on the light, planning your day, anticipating obstacles, and expecting certain outcomes — only to discover that you are a monster. What a miserable fate! One might prefer never to wake up at all.

Some people, undoubtedly, have experiences that leave them with a negative self-image. They see evil and the devil both within themselves and everywhere around them. From what I have observed, such personal affliction often stems from a lack of self-love. Because they do not truly love themselves, they suffer more deeply and are more easily troubled. That being said, I have never encountered anyone who was truly afraid of themselves — not at all. Quite the opposite: Most people desire to be *good* — to be better, more at peace, more serene, healthier, and whole.

Why do we not love ourselves?

At times, we are inclined to look outward — into our neighbor's yard — seeking something we lack, only to find that what we truly need is not there. This happens because we do not know ourselves well enough and, as a result, fail to appreciate our own worth. Socrates taught that the highest good, above all others, is to *know thyself* — to understand oneself and to recognize one's own value.

Through life, as well as through my Christian and priestly experience, I have come to esteem the human person as the first and greatest value — and therefore, I have learned to esteem myself as well. Focusing on oneself is not always *individualism* or *egoism*. On the contrary, one must liberate one's identity, life experiences, wounds, values, and personal potential — if for no other reason than to give thanks to the Creator.

When a person is constantly seeking outside of himself — looking to others or external circumstances for answers — the evil one can take advantage of this restlessness. He inserts himself into that struggle and solitude, exploiting the vulnerability it creates.

To guard against this, it is essential to rediscover a *taste* for the good within us. Self-awareness strengthens and rewards us, making us joyful, exuberant, enthusiastic, optimistic, affable, lovable, benevolent, and generous.

What are the interior conditions for avoiding evil?

I would say that what is needed is deep reflection and, perhaps, a bit of regained focus — if only to recall the pain we last suffered when afflicted by evil, whether through pride or, conversely, through despair.

For this reason, evil is not to be confronted with either the *presumption* of a superhero or the *weakness* of an earthworm.

When faced with evil, there is no alternative: One must remain firmly grounded. If we challenge it recklessly, it becomes fearsome; if we repress it without wisdom, it becomes cowardly. In both cases, evil is ultimately a loser. But if we take it as our standard — engaging it on its own terms — it is victorious. This is because evil understands the necessity of limits, which, when acknowledged, generate the good sense that is the true treasure of those who possess it.

Consider what would happen if world leaders had no limits to their actions — what arrogance and tyranny that would produce! Even they must accept the reality of being merely human, trying to govern as best they can while simply striving to reach old age, which, at best, is a mere hundred years — a rather small sum in the grand scheme of things. Our entire human history is overshadowed by the first couple who were tempted to exceed their proper limits: "You will not die. For God knows that when you eat of it your eyes will be opened, and you will be like God, knowing good and evil" (Gen. 3:4–5).

To revitalize both reason and faith, we must turn to realism, interiority, formation, renewal, hope, and optimism — seeking to train ourselves and safeguard our souls, especially when evil and suffering rage around us. As priests, we must completely abandon empty platitudes, simplistic repressions of suffering, and deceitful spiritual evasions. Instead, we must always speak with clarity and truth, calling white *white* and black *black*.

How can we make this clear to the young?

We must educate them not to swell with pride, yet at the same time, not to become dependent followers. And we must do so in a way that preserves their individuality — preventing them from blindly absorbing the pseudo-values of the mass culture that surrounds them. By training themselves to resist a reductive mentality, they strengthen their own ideas, choices, and positive perspectives, freeing themselves from petty, foolish, and passive opinions.

There is no need to wage war against others. In a stadium, hooligans shout insults at the opposing team — but is it not enough simply to support and cheer for one's own team, encouraging them to victory and not losing heart when they fail? Is that really so difficult to understand?

So many are enslaved by arrogant trends, reinforced by coaches, directors, and journalists who brand them as "bad," "aggressive," and "cynical." What ugly things to say! To be dependent on stupidity is to reveal that one has succumbed to its influence, desperate to be accepted into a cycle of superficial approval. It forces a person to abandon his true self, reducing him to a mere performer — copying, reciting, and playing a role.

The *adult*, on the other hand, does not surrender to popular opinion as though it were an infallible source of truth. Instead, he questions everything, listens carefully, and weighs every word in the attentive and passionate search for even the smallest crumbs of goodness and truth.

The education of the young must be a training in reality, responsibility, limits, and the proper use of freedom — a freedom that remains a true value only when it is directed toward the pursuit of genuine good, both for oneself and for others. This kind of formation enables a person to govern himself — his temperament, character, and habits. Only in this way is true personality cultivated, integrating both natural and acquired virtues, so that each individual may contribute to the betterment of humanity and the world.

How can we "initiate" youth to spiritual combat?

Nature has not placed within them the art of living; they must learn it firsthand, like counting the stars. Experience will take care of the rest, though often at a high price. Parents and teachers prepare them to enter the world — to live, to love, to struggle, and, when the time comes, to die. This is the foundation of all pedagogy, above and beyond any other method of instruction.

Even today, we have tests of maturity — whether in life, in school, or in the workplace. The most common of these are final exams. Yet these trials are no longer characterized by courage and heroism, by personal autonomy, civic responsibility, or the ability to confront adversity. This is why young people across the world feel an instinctive need to *test themselves*, to rediscover archaic initiation rites as a means of entering the world with courage. If the family, society, and community fail to provide them with meaningful *rituals* to mark their passage into maturity, they will invent their own — often with irreversible consequences.

It is dangerous when youth are not prepared to face life, suffering, hardship, and death — realities that modern society improperly represses or attempts to *exorcize*. One need only look at the *emo* subculture, the latest trend among young people. I do not know what the name of this movement means, but I see its adherents wandering with blank expressions, their faces painted and veiled beneath heavy bangs.

By contrast, it is providential to teach young people that evil and the devil exist — realities plainly evident in the world around us. Only then will they understand that sooner or later, they must prepare to confront them. If they are deprived of the necessary formation and indispensable tools to begin, endure, and complete this battle, they will surely lose.

How can we help fathers, mothers, and their children?

The transition between generations must be carefully prepared and gradually planned, free from prejudices about both the past and the future. We must fuse fundamental values and goals with the ongoing process of cultural adaptation so that children receive the dream inherited from their fathers, safeguard it, refine it, and make it their own — before passing it on with passion.

In ancient tribal cultures, the father would lift his newborn child toward heaven — whether male or female — entrusting the infant to God and proclaiming, "Behold, the Only One who is greater than you." In this ritual, he acknowledged the child as *sacred* in relation to himself, to the world, and to the Creator. Through this act of strength and blessing, he prepared the child to one day assume leadership — to fortify the tribe against external threats and contribute to its flourishing. In this way, the youth was equipped to oppose evil and the wicked spirit that embodies it.

It was the community that initiated the young into the hunt. At the age of twelve, after learning the skill from his elders, a boy was given a bow and arrows and sent alone into the heart of the forest for six months. If he returned victorious, he was welcomed, honored, and inducted into the ranks of the warriors. If he did not return, the tribe would search for him: If he was found lost, he was brought back and assigned to tend the livestock — the only role deemed suitable for him. If he had fallen, his body was carried home on the shoulders of his tribesmen and honored as a victorious warrior.

Thus, they celebrated not only those who triumphed over their prey or their enemies, but also those who fell in the struggle — so long as they had first done their part in preparing for the fight.

Is it possible to attain such objectives in a world such as ours?

In both society and the family, there is often a tendency to dismantle the archetypal values of the generations that came before us. If, from infancy, we have been subjected to conformist influences — alienated and depersonalized by passing trends — we must not become demoralized or waste time blaming our parents, society, or anything else. Instead, we must rise again and conform ourselves to reality. By remaining faithful to reality, we will ultimately be victorious. Just as reality makes us suffer, so too does it bring us joy; just as it causes us to lose, so too does it enable us to win. Hardships, when faced with all our strength — without distraction or misguided intentions — do not have the power to destroy us. The first act of patience, then, is to begin again: to return to our origins in order to recognize and reclaim our personal, natural, and acquired values.

Those who undertake and succeed in this are *purebreds* — men and women of the highest quality, strong and resolute souls, motivated and steadfast in their growth. This is not about recovering something lost, but about rediscovering our own identity, personal worth, wisdom, and mastery over our thoughts and our lives.

"Seeing us concentrated on God, our highest good, the devil grows weary and retreats."

CHAPTER TEN

Prepared and Ready

"Therefore, take the whole armor of God, that you may be able to withstand the evil day, and having done all, to stand."[27]

What are the interior dispositions needed to avoid demonic influences?

The first step is to seek help in *interiorizing* whatever distress we may feel within ourselves. This distress can manifest in many ways: sadness, anger, violence, rebellion, even blasphemy. In reality, we do not immediately perceive ourselves as *bad*, but rather as wounded and suffering. It is our right, therefore, to free ourselves from this deep unrest and affliction.

The second step is to abandon attitudes of indifference, apathy, and disinterest toward the good. Instead, we must strive to live with profound serenity and a clear conscience, so that when we go to bed at the end of the day, we find ourselves at peace — within ourselves, in body and soul, with those around us, and with God, the source of all true good.

Communion with God is indispensable. For this reason, we must turn away from practical atheism, abandon a life of sin, and progress toward a life in God. It is essential to free ourselves from the devil's deceptions, which manifest in many *idols* that oppress us. Here, we shall attempt to name some of them. But above all, one

---

[27] Ephesians 6:13.

must will to be absolutely free from evil, renouncing Satan and all his works.

The more one dwells in God (*for it is the Lord who liberates and protects*), the more secure and free one becomes. This requires humility, faith, and prayer — not only on the part of individuals but also within families. The daily recitation of the Rosary, frequent reception of the Sacraments (*especially the Eucharist and the Sacrament of Reconciliation*), a Christian life in full conformity with the Gospel, works of charity, and the forgiveness of one's enemies — all these are essential in the battle against evil.

Are there any tricks for spiting the devil?

If there is a way to deflect the devil from us, it is by allowing ourselves to be drawn toward the goodness and beauty that emanate from what is good — and from God, our Father. It is this attraction to the Lord that *distracts* us from the seductions of the evil one, leading us instead toward life, toward what is good, toward others, and toward the highest human values. It enables us to overcome the malicious temptations that incite anger, violence, and division — sources of profound suffering. By following this golden thread that leads to divine wonder, we wayfarers come upon a table richly prepared with a banquet. We stop, eat, and drink, becoming fully satisfied — unaware at times of the beast lurking nearby, though dressed in splendor, waiting in ambush. The fallen angel persistently attempts to harass us, but seeing that our hearts and minds are fixed upon God, our highest good, he grows weary, retreats with his tail between his legs, and slinks away in defeat.

How does one notice the tracks of the devil?

As I have mentioned, even today, many believe that certain absurdities and evil actions defy explanation unless one acknowledges the presence of the devil. People attribute to him, for example, the arrogance and manipulation of cynical minds that shape public opinion for commercial gain, or the exploitation of adolescent instincts as a source of profit for those peddling eroticism. Many evils, as I have said, are ascribed to the devil.

The Gospel is precise in distinguishing between illness and demonic possession, even if their outward effects can sometimes appear identical. On the one hand, we must not be too quick to assume demonic influence; on the other, we must remain vigilant in uncovering the devil's tricks, particularly the ways in which he conceals his actions.

The most common sign of demonic influence is an aversion to the sacred — such as when someone suddenly finds themselves unable to pray or grows irritable when hearing prayers at home. This is especially concerning when it happens to someone who was previously devout and practicing, only to abruptly cut ties with faith and, in some cases, begin to blaspheme.

This kind of aversion manifests in various ways, often accompanied by converging signs. For example, if a priest arrives to bless a house and someone reacts irrationally — locking the door, shutting themselves in their room, or refusing to open — it may indicate a deeper spiritual disturbance.

Holy water is sometimes used for *diagnostic* purposes, as are exorcised oil and incense, to observe whether an individual exhibits an extreme repulsion to sacred objects and rites. In some cases, those under demonic influence react violently to these elements — especially when they are unaware of their presence.

Other specific signs of demonic affliction include extraordinary physical strength, such as the ability to break objects — even iron chains. Unexplained noises, particularly at night, are also common. The afflicted individual may become agitated, shout uncontrollably, and display wild, blasphemous behavior — only to later have no memory of the episode. At times, the person may suddenly become so unnaturally heavy that they cannot be lifted, even by several people.

So it's indispensable to entrust oneself to God, to Our Lady, and to the saints.

To avoid falling under the power of the devil, one must stand firmly on the side of God, Our Lady, the saints, and the good in all its forms. This requires an awareness of one's sacred dignity and value, as well as a refusal to anchor oneself to corrupt powers — whether ideological, economic, political, or the pseudo-religious deceptions that ultimately prove toxic.

Beyond the exercise of good sense, realism, and prudence in recognizing any direct actions of the tempter in their various forms, we must place all our trust in the Lord, clinging to Him, our defender and protector. Above all, the Christian surrenders himself to God through prayer.

At the end of the nineteenth century, a young woman from the French middle class, St. Thérèse of Lisieux, rose to the mystical heights of Catherine of Siena and embraced the *folly* of the Cross in the spirit of St. John of the Cross. In her prayer, she cried out:

> You are the Eagle whom I love and who draws me upward! You, who, plunging into this land of exile, chose to suffer and die to steal away souls and immerse them in the heart of the Holy Trinity, that eternal fire of love. ... Allow me to say that Your love reaches the point of folly! How could I not desire that, in the face of such divine madness, my own love would soar toward You? Ah! I know that for You, the saints have embraced madness, and my own folly is the hope that Your love will receive me as its victim. ... Adorable Eagle, I shall remain for as long as You will, fixed upon You, gazing eye to eye. I long to be dazzled![28]

[28] St. Thérèse of the Child Jesus, *Manuscript B*, 262, in *Complete Works* (Vatican City: LEV-OCD, 1997), 228.

What an immense contrast between the *cruel* and *rapacious* eagle — symbol of the devil — and the divine Eagle, Jesus Christ, who "desired to suffer and die to draw all souls" into the heart of the Father.[29] As Scripture says, God is "like an eagle that stirs up its nest, that hovers over its young" (Deut. 32:11).

How can we live daily this surrender to God?

To stand firm against the devil, one must daily savor the tenderness of God the Father, much as the saints did in their lives. Divine love is concentrated in the rich fruits of Christian life — through the assimilation of God's word, the memorial and celebration of salvation in the Church's liturgy, and the daily witness of Christian Faith.

A Christian who fully embraces the spiritual patrimony of the Church will not, even when faced with inexplicable or incurable afflictions, resort to magicians or fortune-tellers. He sees such practices as vain and illusory, in radical contradiction to the gift of faith.

This steadfastness in faith and witness can itself become a sign of Christian hope, offering those still lost amid the rise of evil a fuller sense of existence and communion with God.

Despite everything, the Christian knows that, in God's name and through hope and optimism, the devil and his followers can be overcome — even today — through an unwavering passion for goodness. I do not believe that, in order to rediscover these *placid waters,* to savor and delight in what is good, one must come to any *agreement* with the devil, who is diametrically opposed to it.

What do you mean concretely?

The Word of God exhorts us to sobriety and fortitude, to vigilance and prayer, so that we may be prepared for battle and overcome the evil one.

[29] Ibid.

The Apostle Paul's own struggle against the powers of evil is well known. He reminds us, for example, of how he opposed the evil spirit that sought to hinder his apostolic journey to Thessalonica: "Because we wanted to come to you — I, Paul, again and again — but Satan hindered us" (1 Thess. 2:18).

He shares this warning to make Christians aware of the devil's power of seduction, which he knows well — but the devil also knows him: "Jesus I know, and Paul I know; but who are you?" (Acts 19:15), the adversarial spirit asked a group of Jewish exorcists, before violently attacking them, stripping them, and sending them fleeing at the hands of a demon-possessed man.

What spiritual "weapons" does the Christian possess?

According to St. Paul, Christians possess, above all, the grace of God to engage the enemy on equal ground. In a private revelation, the Apostle is reassured: "My grace is sufficient for you" (2 Cor. 12:9). By that point, he had fought the good fight of faith and urged his disciple Timothy to act as "a good soldier of Christ Jesus" (2 Tim. 2:3). Likewise, he exhorted the communities he evangelized to arm themselves spiritually, reminding them, "You have not yet resisted to the point of shedding your blood" (Heb. 12:4).

Paul frequently ends his letters with calls to strength, steadfastness, and vigilance. In his Letter to the Ephesians, he expands on this theme, writing in a time of intense persecution against God's chosen ones and divisions among Christians. Having already urged the baptized to strip off the *old self* enslaved to evil, he now exhorts them to *put on the armor of God* so that they may withstand the devil's power. In doing so, he assures them that God Himself fights on their side. Strengthened and equipped in this way — "having put on the breastplate of righteousness ... and taken the helmet of salvation" (Eph. 6:14, 17) — the Christian can prevail against his *celestial* adversaries, who would otherwise overpower him by their superior nature, intelligence, and strategy.

Paul outlines the various defensive weapons available to believers, using the terminology of the Roman legions: the belt of truth, the breastplate of righteousness, the footgear for proclaiming the Gospel of peace, the shield of faith, the helmet of salvation, and the double-edged sword of the Word of God. He makes clear that these divine gifts are not only meant for personal edification but are also essential for defense and for victory in the battle against evil.

He concludes by exhorting Christians to constant prayer — the greatest of all spiritual weapons — not merely in the morning, at midday, and in the evening, but without ceasing. Prayer, made possible by the inspiration of the Holy Spirit, is to be offered for the entire Christian community, "for all the saints" — that is, for the whole Church — and especially for Paul himself. Imprisoned in chains, he hopes for the opportunity to once again proclaim the Gospel boldly, convinced that its preaching must be upheld by the Church's intercession against the devil, the ultimate adversary.

The Apostle, who had already emphasized the meekness of the Master in the face of His adversaries, warns his readers to remain vigilant against the diabolical enemy, "who prowls like a roaring lion, seeking someone to devour" (1 Pet. 5:8).

What explicit means can we make use of?

Several effective means are regularly used to keep the deceits and ploys of the devil at bay, as well as to aid in liberating souls from Satan's power. These must be used with faith and in conjunction with other means of grace.

Holy water, or exorcised water, is widely employed in many liturgical rites. Its significance is directly linked to the baptismal rite, where the prayer of blessing over the water invokes the Lord's protection: the forgiveness of sins, defense against the seductions of the evil one, divine safeguarding, deliverance from demonic powers, the increase of divine grace, and protection from all harmful influences in people's homes. Holy water can be sprinkled but may also be imbibed.

Exorcised oil similarly exerts beneficial effects when applied with faith. Beyond promoting bodily health, it serves as a safeguard against adversities, illnesses, curses, and other demonic influences, frustrating the assaults of the devil and the specters he arouses. In many cases, it is used to anoint the body, though it may also be applied to food consumed by individuals afflicted by curses.

Incense is another effective means of protection. As recounted in the book of Tobit, its fragrance drives demons away: "Then the demon will smell it and flee away, and will never again return" (Tob. 6:17).

Exorcised salt is particularly useful for casting out demons, especially in cleansing environments. It is often spread at the entrance of a house or in the four corners of a room suspected of being infested.

Can you explain the Medal of St. Benedict?

The Medal of St. Benedict of Nursia is widely used, along with the Crucifix of Peaceful Death, a medallion that serves as a reminder of St. Benedict's legendary death. According to tradition, he passed away standing near the altar, hands raised heavenward, after having received Holy Communion.

The medal gained widespread popularity from the 11th century onward, thanks to the work of Pope St. Leo IX, himself a Benedictine monk. Later, Pope Benedict XIV definitively established its design, which bears the following inscriptions:

1. ***Front side:*** An image of St. Benedict holding a cross in his hand.

2. ***Reverse side:*** A cross surrounded by a series of Latin initials representing a powerful prayer:

> **C. S. P. B.** — *Crux Sancti Patris Benedicti* (The Cross of the Holy Father Benedict).
>
> **C. S. S. M. L.** — *Crux Sacra Sit Mihi Lux* (May the Holy Cross Be My Light).
>
> **N. D. S. M. D.** — *Non Draco Sit Mihi Dux* (Let Not the Devil Be My Guide).
>
> **V. R. S.** — *Vade Retro, Satana* (Begone, Satan!).
>
> **N. S. M. V.** — *Non Suade Mihi Vana* (Do Not Tempt Me with Vain Things).
>
> **S. M. Q. L.** — *Sunt Mala Quae Libas* (What You Offer Is Evil).
>
> **I. V. B.** — *Ipse Venena Bibas* (Drink Your Own Poison).

The serpent emerging from a chalice depicted on the medal recalls a famous miracle attributed to St. Benedict. According to legend, his enemies attempted to poison him by offering him a cup of poisoned wine. When he made the sign of the cross over the goblet, it *shattered instantly*, saving his life. The final initials of the prayer refer directly to this event.

How can one believe in an infinitely good God and simultaneously believe in the existence of the devil and the eternity of hell?

We shall attempt to respond to this complex question by following the guidance of Sacred Scripture, where the ultimate and eternal realities of life after death are revealed and illuminated.

Today, tolerance and the abolition of the death penalty are increasingly defended, just as the notion of incarceration as a deterrent or instrument of punishment is being replaced with the idea of re-education and rehabilitation for the guilty.

At first glance, it might seem that we have become more merciful than God, given that hell — with all its interminable grief — remains eternally unbridgeable, separating the Creator from His creatures who are condemned to eternal punishment. Yet even Moses once pleaded with God, "Blot me, I pray Thee, out of Thy book" (Exod. 32:32), offering himself to perdition if God would not show mercy to his brethren by forgiving their sins. Similarly, St. Paul expressed a willingness to suffer the same fate: "For I could wish that I myself were accursed and cut off from Christ for the sake of my brethren" (Rom. 9:3).

In recent times, several scholars have reopened this debate with renewed enthusiasm, asserting their hope in a universal salvation. The Orthodox theologian Paul Evdokimov held the view that "those who think that, besides themselves, even just one other person could be eternally lost can no longer love without reservation. … Love hopes all things … such unlimited hope is not only permitted, it is appropriate."

Yet the suffering of existence and the eternal persistence of the devil do not undermine the edifice of goodness, whose source is God Himself, the felicitous source par excellence. The unavoidable damnation of the devil and the eternity of hell reveal what might be called the "impotence of God" before human freedom — the power to choose life or death. A person intoxicated with the drug of evil to the point of losing himself cannot be saved by anyone unless he himself desires salvation. This is no facile alibi or infantile loophole; it is, rather, a harsh reality. Just as it is exceedingly difficult for a person to free himself from the paralysis of substance addiction, so too is it impossible for another to liberate him against his will. Those on the outside remain impotent and unarmed, for only the afflicted can choose to be saved. This is why it is imperative to learn how to use one's freedom wisely — for those unprepared or irresponsible risk destroying not only themselves but everything around them.

For this reason, hell is not a cosmic concentration camp, but the voluntary rejection of God — a free and conscious decision to remain eternally separated from Him. As Ladislaus Boros put it, "Thus, at the moment the damned tries to repent for his deed, he would find himself in heaven. But it is precisely this that he does not want. And hell is precisely this."

Giorgio Gozzelino, a biblical scholar, likewise explains:

> Hell should not be understood as supplementary information about the afterlife. Nor as a tragic utterance without hope — "Behold what will happen to wicked men!" Rather, it is a proclamation: "Behold what must absolutely not happen to anyone, that which all must fight against at the cost of any sacrifice."

He further clarifies that purgatory "is not a shortened version of hell, nor hell with a limited sentence, but rather a growth in friendship with the Lord that continues after death, comparable to mystical knowledge obtained through a struggle consisting of darkness and light. Purification would be something analogous, but always within the joy of eternal communion with God."

It is far better, then, to endure purgatory here in this life rather than in the afterlife.

In what way does the existence of the devil and hell arouse or extinguish Christian hope?

The existence of the devil inaugurates a "robust" Christian pedagogy, one without complexes, because it engages with reality — evil, justice, freedom, reward and punishment, death and life. The devil can also instill fear by using hell as a deterrent, which might give rise to a fear complex. Nonetheless, the fact that he exists and is at work serves even more as an incentive to invest in life, with all its terrible and absurd events — both easy and complicated, yet still stupendous. In this struggle, all of us should allow ourselves to be drawn in and loved by Our Lord, precisely because the angel of darkness is always lurking, ready to confuse evil with good.

The Christian cultivates a sense of hope, rooted in the credible content of the ultimate realities — blessed eternity already breaking into history, inaugurated in the present life by the Paschal event of the Resurrection and life of Jesus Christ. In Him, the triumph of good over evil, love over hatred, and life over death is made manifest. The judgment of the Cross and the Resurrection of Christ lays bare the presence of evil in human history, where it is incarnated and active in the devil and hell, but also affirms the beatifying presence and action of God, of the good, of purification, and of paradise.

Why did Jesus not liberate Judas from Satan?

God does not impose His gifts, not even the gift of salvation and eternal life, because He esteems us as His sons and does not treat us as servants. The Son of God made man respected the liberty of Judas, even though the hard-hearted traitor used that freedom against Him and against himself. Who knows how many times the Lord tried to transform his heart into a heart of flesh? "Our brother Judas," as Fr. Primo Mazzolari put it, was more than the other apostles in the heart of Christ, who went to His death above all for His betrayer, after that kiss in the Garden of Gethsemane.

How can one turn a diabolical experience into something positive and useful?

God never desires evil, although He allows it even when it is the creature who desires it. I can pay an assassin to kill a person. God is not bound to impede him, because to the victim who has died bodily, God assures eternal life after all that he has suffered. We often do not consider this "final victory" of God over the power of evil and death.

He never rejects His creatures, even in Satan's case when he separated himself from the Creator and was cast down to earth. In the end, however, it is always God who keeps the books. He knows how to draw good from evil. How can we understand this?

It seems inevitable that at times we need to be profoundly humiliated in order to recognize that our point of departure was mistaken, that our understanding of our own and others' good was extremely limited. The humiliation of trials and defeats suffered leads to effacing our presumption and putting our presuppositions in doubt. At any rate, terrible physical or interior suffering, even when it is innocent affliction that we have not provoked, once overcome and illuminated, becomes a source of great hope: In the final analysis, "life is not taken away, but transformed."

Can one be a Catholic without believing in the existence of the devil?

Paragraph 11 of the conciliar decree *Unitatis Redintegratio* states that theologians, "when comparing doctrines with one another, should remember that in Catholic doctrine there exists a 'hierarchy' of truths, since they vary in their relation to the fundamental Christian Faith." The greater or lesser closeness of revealed or ecclesial doctrine to the heart of the Christian mystery and to the history of salvation thus becomes a criterion for establishing a certain order and weight in the truths of the Faith. The doctrine regarding the devil is not found at the forefront of the hierarchy of truths, though it is neither marginal nor false; rather, Sacred Scripture and the Catholic Church consider it necessary for teaching our contemporaries an awareness of the disturbing power of evil and of the superhuman being that incarnates it in history.

How can we speak to children about evil, the devil, hell, and paradise?

Is there a need to do so? At any rate, though they are at the start of their lives, they already perceive the effects of hell everywhere — perhaps even in their families.

If it must be done, I would tell of a mouth-watering experience — not to children, but to their parents: A holy man one day had the opportunity to converse with God and asked Him, "Lord, I would like to know what heaven and hell are like."

God led the holy man toward two doors. He opened one and let him look inside.

There, he saw an enormous round table. In the middle of the table sat a huge platter of food with a delicious aroma. The holy man felt his mouth water. The people seated around the table, however, were thin, bruised, and sickly in appearance. They all looked famished. Each had a spoon with an impossibly long handle attached to their arms. Though they could reach the food and scoop it up, the spoon handles were too long to bring the food to their mouths. The holy man trembled at the sight of their misery and suffering. God said, "You have just seen hell."

God then led the man to the second door and opened it. The scene inside was identical: the great round table, the same enticing platter of food, and the same people with long-handled spoons attached to their arms. Yet this time, the people were well-fed, smiling, and conversing joyfully. The holy man asked God, "I don't understand!"

God replied, "It is simple. These people have learned to feed one another. The first group, on the other hand, think only of themselves. The difference between hell and paradise is made by those who do not allow themselves to be loved by Me so that each may love the other in turn."

Thus spoke Our Lord to the good man.

This is what parents should tell their children.

What will become of the devil?

As for the final destiny of Satan, it has been revealed that "the God of peace will soon crush Satan" (Rom. 16:20) under the feet of the elect. "And then the lawless one will be revealed, and the Lord Jesus will slay him with the breath of His mouth and destroy him by His appearing and His coming" (2 Thess. 2:8), that is, by His glory. Satan and his angels will be cast out forever.

In his book *The Devil*, Giovanni Papini affirms the ancient idea of the *apocatastasis*, or the final reconciliation of all beings in God, and adds that the task of human beings would be that of converting the devil: "Could it be that Christ," writes Papini, "might have wanted to free us from slavery to the devil also in the hope that men, in turn, might liberate the devil from his condemnation? Could it be that Christ might have redeemed men so that they, by means of His precept commanding the love of enemies, might be worthy to dream one day the redemption of His most menacing and proud Enemy?"

Well, it is an extraordinary prospect. Certainly, it is necessary to stay far from the devil as long as he remains what he is: infernal, wrathful, filled with hatred against God and against all; just as we should stay far away from Freemasonry, the mafia, drugs, and things of this sort which represent the devil. Nevertheless, how comforting it would be to see him fall not into the infernal abyss but into the heart of God in eternity! We would all gladly clap our hands and approach him and be able to contemplate him as he was destined to be and ought to return to being: Lucifer, the bearer of the reflected divine light. For this to happen depends solely upon him, because I imagine that the good God would be quite happy to welcome him, transformed in this way, into His Fatherly heart.

*Fr. Amorth has written many articles in various
periodicals edited by the Society of St. Paul.*

Profile and Evaluation

Biographical Profile of Fr. Gabriele Amorth

Born on May 1, 1925, the last of five male children, he received an excellent upbringing in his family, profoundly religious, and then in his parish. He graduated from a classical high school, where he played sports (fencing and volleyball) and acted in the parish theater. At that time, many parishes had a thespian club. During the War of Liberation, he fought in the Italian Brigade, the Catholic formation of partisans, and was awarded the Cross of Valor as a recognition for the following reasons: "From the very beginning he dedicated himself to the clandestine struggle of resistance showing himself a wise organizer, intelligent informer and intrepid combatant. Captured three times, he succeeded in regaining his liberty with great ability and although threatened with death, persisted undaunted in his activities, contributing effectively to victory."

In 1945, he entered the Christian Democratic Party, and took part in the first provincial committee, in charge of youth; he was called to Rome by his professor and friend Giuseppe Dossetti, who had him nominated delegate national assistant of Christian Democrat youth. The head delegate was Giulio Andreotti, but Gabriele did everything because Andreotti was completely occupied with De Gasperi. When he entered the administration, he saw that he would be nominated a national delegate but preferred to renounce the post: He had realized he no longer wanted to enter politics but become a priest.

From 1942 to 1968 he frequented Padre Pio of Pietrelcina, later proclaimed a saint by Pope John Paul II. In 1947, he obtained his degree in jurisprudence and entered the Society of St. Paul. For some years he had been in contact with the founder of the Society of St. Paul, a priest from Piedmont, Fr. Giacomo Alberione (1884–1971), who would be proclaimed blessed by Pope John Paul II. He was ordained a priest on January 24, 1954, by Msgr. Roatta. He carried out teaching roles, preaching, and wrote many articles for various periodicals edited by the Society of St. Paul. Fr. Amorth was, in fact, a professional journalist.

From 1958 to 1959, he had one of the most beautiful experiences of his life. He thought the moment had come to consecrate Italy to the Immaculate Heart of Mary. He immediately received the enthusiastic approval of the Bologna Cardinal Giacomo Lercaro; the initiative was then shared by the Italian Bishops' Conference. He was named organizational secretary for the event and had to fight against the tight deadlines set for preparing the Italian public: The date was set for September 13, 1959, on the occasion of the National Eucharistic Congress. Together with others, he planned a great *Peregrinatio Mariae*. The statue of Our Lady of Fatima was brought from Portugal, and an itinerary in a helicopter was organized with stops in all the provincial capitals. The initiative was a great success.

As director of the monthly *Madre di Dio* (*Mother of God*), he wrote many articles and six books on the Virgin Mary, taking great interest then in the apparitions in Medjugorje. He was given various leadership roles in his Congregation.

It was Padre Pio who set the young Gabriele (in the photo to the right of Padre Pio, already ordained a priest) on the path to join the Society of St. Paul.

In 1986, his work took a profound change of direction when Cardinal Ugo Poletti nominated him as an exorcist of Rome. For him, it was an entirely new world. He saw the great scarcity of exorcists and, under the guidance of the Passionist priest Fr. Candido Diamantini, he took his ministry in two directions: doing exorcisms and making bishops and priests aware of this need, which was neither believed nor perceived.

His natural combative character, which won him a medal of honor in the military, rendered him capable of opposing adequately and tenaciously the angel of darkness, the enemy of God and of men. He would counter him even with the unusual weapon of the sneer, denigration, and the classic mocking, because "the best way of casting out the devil if he does not want to give in to the texts of Scripture," Luther held, "is to deride and insult him because he cannot bear to be ridiculed." And Thomas More added that "the devil … that prowde spirit …, cannot endure to be mocked."[30] Fr. Gabriele Amorth confronts the devil holding in his right hand a large crucifix of St. Benedict (12 x 6 in) and sticks out his tongue with a grimace, irritating him and putting him to flight.

---

[30]   In C. S. Lewis, *The Screwtape Letters* (New York: HarperCollins, 2001), 5.

*Intensely devoted to Our Lady of Fatima, Fr. Gabriele
begins every exorcism invoking her protection.*

Attempts at an Evaluation

As concerns Fr. Amorth's work as an exorcist, there have been several controversies. Some suspect that he has not revealed the full truth about the devil. For example, one cardinal reportedly told him, "You are an exorcist, but we both know that Satan does not exist, right? All superstition. Come on, you wouldn't have me think that you really believe that?"[31]

He has also faced opposition from mainstream media, particularly for his criticisms of Freemasonry and its powerful adherents. It has been documented that Freemasonry presents itself as a "religion," an alternative to Christianity, using innumerable symbols and secret ceremonies to exalt Lucifer as the "god of light," the rebel angel at work behind the events of the modern world.[32] In doing so, it even draws on texts from the Old and New Testaments, distorting them to promote a confused religious syncretism that is both neopagan and esoteric.

Thomas Paine, a known Freemason, once stated, "We all know that the Sun is the fountain of light, the source of the seasons, the cause of the succession of days and nights, the sustenance of vegetation, the friend of man. Therefore, only the wise Freemason knows why the Sun is placed in the center of this beautiful hall."[33]

The cult of the sun, celebrated by the ancients, was symbolized by the O — the "center," the "eye," the "solar wheel that moves everything," the "sacred fire" of secret rites. Modern Freemasonry has adopted this symbolism in its essential form.

Fr. Amorth was outspoken against Freemasonry, declaring: "The one in charge is the one with the money. Our world is managed

---

[31] Stefano Lorenzetto, *Il Giornale*, March 19, 2013.

[32] Angela Musolesi, *Experiences and Elucidations of Fr. Gabriele Amorth* (Città di Castello: Edizioni Carismatici Francescani, 2005), 134.

[33] Thomas Paine, *An Essay on the Origin of Freemasonry* (New York, 1818).

Seeing Fr. Amorth sticking out his tongue, the devil finds no escape.

by seven or eight people who hold all the cash."[34] He did not soften his stance when discussing certain Italian politicians, whom he described as Freemasons. *Avvenire*, the daily of the Italian Bishops' Conference, once pointed out that even Montecitorio, the square in front of the Italian Parliament, is "embellished with an abundant series of 'five-pointed stars,'[35] the most important and universally

---

[34] Stefano Lorenzetto, *Il Giornale*, March 19, 2013.

[35] From the issue of June 26, 1987, on page 7. The five-pointed star is considered by Freemasonry to be a representation "of Harmony and Brotherhood," but in reality it is the sun god of the ancient Pythagoreans. In the setting of

recognized symbol of Freemasonry."[36] In 1871, the Italian state extended the presence of this shining star, replacing the Savoia cross on military uniforms with the Masonic emblem.

Lucifer, the sun demon, is often symbolized by a dot within a circle, a shining star, or the number 666 — each associated with solar imagery. Variations of this triad appear frequently. It is notable, for instance, that three discreetly placed sixes were imprinted on the frontispiece of Galileo's *Dialogue*, a work infamously linked to sun worship. Today, Masonic symbols are embedded in barcodes, logos, flags, and banknotes. The American dollar is laden with them, as is the Euro.

Even Christian tradition has been infiltrated by this imagery. Crucifixes, for example, often feature the shining star. Official breviaries of the Catholic Church use a five-pointed star as an asterisk in the Psalms — pointing upward in the Luciferian sense — despite Times New Roman's convention of rendering the asterisk with six points. In the *Te Deum*, this star is encased in a red circle, akin to the O, marking the start of an optional stanza.

One may also question why the church in San Giovanni Rotondo, dedicated to Padre Pio, was built in a spiral rather than the traditional Latin cross. This design choice, allegedly made in deference to architect Renzo Piano's "sincere religiosity" (Crispino Valenziano), reflects not Christian symbolism but the secular, anti-supernatural spirit of the modern world (K. W. Forster). In Christian tradition, the spiral holds no significance. In

---

initiation, it is the opposite symbol to the cross, ever more invasive, though less and less opposed. The shining star with flaming points is Lucifer himself. Interestingly, it is also defined as the Sacred Number of the sun, 666: the number of the antichrist and mark of the beast in Revelation.

[36] Epiphanius, *Freemasonry and Secret Sects: The Hidden Side of History* (n.p.: n.d.), 193. See also *Chiesa Viva* 33, no. 381 (March 2006).

Freemasonry, however, it represents the Great Architect of the Universe, the dynamic principle of the cosmos, associated with Fire, Light, Life, Struggle, Effort, Thought, Conscience, Progress, Civilization, Liberty, and Independence — all culminating in the assertion that "Satan is God, the only God of our planet" (H. P. Blavatsky). Albert Pike, a leading Masonic authority, likewise affirmed: "The Masonic religion must be maintained in the purity of its Luciferian doctrine. Yes, Lucifer is God, the true and pure philosophical religion is faith in Lucifer against Adonai." The spiral also signifies the Masonic path of initiation, a passage from earth to heaven through Gnosis, which leads to man's self-deification.

Naturally, this deeper meaning is concealed. Instead, the public is fed banal explanations: the church is a "spider," an "open space," a "high-tech marvel," a "shell" cradling Padre Pio, the "pearl" inside.

In the churchyard stand eight sculpted eagles in flight. While the eagle holds positive symbolism in Christianity, it also has a darker meaning, signifying predatory power and oppression. The 30th degree of Freemasonry features an eagle with two heads and raised wings; the 32nd degree displays two such eagles; the 33rd degree presents a single eagle with two heads. Adding these together, we arrive at eight — the precise number found in the churchyard.

At the 30th degree, the Freemason publicly declares war on God, offering a sacrifice to Lucifer (Baphomet) and shaking his dagger toward heaven, invoking: "Lucifer, Holy God, Vindicator!" He then curses Adonai, exclaiming, "Revenge, Adonai!" The 32nd degree, often called the Hebrew degree, represents exile, suffering, and vengeance — not only the suffering of the Israelites wandering the desert but also Lucifer's rebellion and fall. Here, the initiate embraces the Great Pantheistic Falsehood of the eternal transformation of the universe, leading to man's self-deification and the construction of a new Tower of Babel — the foundation of a one-world Masonic religion. The 33rd degree completes the arc: All religions and authorities must be annihilated, replaced with the Luciferian Order, which spreads moral chaos, subverts consciences, and imposes its doctrine on families, nations, and the world through audacity, deception, and violence.

Given this, is it any wonder that evil and the Evil One enter the Church itself? Satan delights in sowing confusion, especially where the Source of all Good — Our Lord in the Eucharist — is found. The devil does not trouble the papal court, corrupt clergy, or lukewarm Christians; in fact, he appreciates them. His greatest enemy is the Eucharist, along with those who adore It.

Poor Padre Pio was tormented by the devil in life, but his greatest trial may have come after death. The architectural aberration built in his honor stands as a grotesque mockery of his sanctity. Thankfully, the faithful who visit the site remain unaware of its Masonic significance. Once again, the devil's handiwork can run, but it cannot hide.

Modern society is inundated with solar and Masonic symbolism — woven into advertising, logos, and the objects we use daily. This symbolic manipulation, largely subliminal, is designed to imprint psychological "energy drains," forge psychic bonds, and condition the masses. Though dismissed as irrational by skeptics, these strategies are anything but imaginary.

To counter this, we must educate ourselves on these deceptions. Only by recognizing and understanding them can we resist their influence.

C. S. Lewis famously wrote:

> There are two equal and opposite errors into which our race can fall about the devils. One is to disbelieve in their existence. The other is to believe, and to feel an excessive

and unhealthy interest in them. They themselves are equally pleased by both errors and hail a materialist or a magician with the same delight.[37]

Those who wish to avoid both pitfalls must educate themselves on the devil's tactics, which are deliberately veiled and secret. The enemy thrives on ignorance and complacency.

Fr. Gabriele is now living in the infirmary of the community he belongs to, attending to the many letters he receives.

[37]   C. S. Lewis, *The Screwtape Letters* (New York: HarperCollins, 2001), ix.

About the Author

Fr. Gabriele Amorth (1925–2016), the most famous Italian exorcist, was ordained a priest in 1954. In 1985, he became an exorcist for the Diocese of Rome, a ministry he practiced until his death. In 1990, he founded the International Association of Exorcists, of which he was president until 2000. He wrote more than thirty books in Italian, many of which have been translated into other languages.

Sophia Institute

SOPHIA INSTITUTE IS A nonprofit institution that seeks to nurture the spiritual, moral, and cultural life of souls and to spread the gospel of Christ in conformity with the authentic teachings of the Roman Catholic Church.

Sophia Institute Press fulfills this mission by offering translations, reprints, and new publications that afford readers a rich source of the enduring wisdom of mankind.

Sophia Institute also operates the popular online resource CatholicExchange.com. *Catholic Exchange* provides world news from a Catholic perspective as well as daily devotionals and articles that will help readers to grow in holiness and live a life consistent with the teachings of the Church.

In 2013, Sophia Institute launched Sophia Institute for Teachers to renew and rebuild Catholic culture through service to Catholic education. With the goal of nurturing the spiritual, moral, and cultural life of souls, and an abiding respect for the role and work of teachers, we strive to provide materials and programs that are at once enlightening to the mind and ennobling to the heart; faithful and complete, as well as useful and practical.

Sophia Institute gratefully recognizes the Solidarity Association for preserving and encouraging the growth of our apostolate over the course of many years. Without their generous and timely support, this book would not be in your hands.

www.SophiaInstitute.com
www.CatholicExchange.com
www.SophiaTeachers.org

Sophia Institute Press is a registered trademark of Sophia Institute.
Sophia Institute is a tax-exempt institution as defined by the
Internal Revenue Code, Section 501(c)(3). Tax ID 22-2548708.